Grilling with
Chef George Hirsch

Grilling with
Chef George Hirsch

George Hirsch with Marie Bianco

Hearst Books / New York

Dedicated to the memory of

Pauline L. Hirsch, my first teacher, who "knew her fire" and

who taught me to "know my fire"

Library of Congress Cataloging-in-Publication Data

Hirsch, George.
    Grilling with chef George Hirsch / by George Hirsch with Marie Bianco.
      p. cm.
    Includes index.
    ISBN 0-688-13553-6
    1. Barbecue cookery. I. Bianco, Marie. II. Title.
TX840.B3H56 1994
641.5'784—dc20   93-46016
                                              CIP

Printed in the United States of America

First Edition

1 2 3 4 5 6 7 8 9 10

BOOK DESIGN BY RICHARD ORIOLO

Acknowledgments

With my sincerest appreciation to:

Marie Bianco, for making my creative thoughts and recipes fun during the writing of this book, and for reminding me why I am a chef—for our love of food and to make people smile.

Dan Kossoff, who "knows his focus"—a giant of a person, friend, director, gourmand, and golfer . . . not necessarily in that order.

Arlene Wong, whose dedication to "building the fire" has set a new standard for all chefs to follow.

Peter Gassiraro, for always being available and knowing the facts of the fire.

WJCT and Whitehawk Pictures, Jacksonville, Florida, and to all my new friends there who cheered me through each chapter and each show.

Carol, Jack, Norm, Steve, and Tom, the best production crew—with or without the fire.

The Charbroil team: Tim, Ron, and all—and especially Gay Goodnite, for making it easy to grill and "know your fire."

Mickey Rotella, who always kept the candles burning for the fire.

George J. Hirsch, my best friend, who gives me the strength to build the fire and for always applauding the fruits of my fire.

Dori M. Hirsch, an endless fire of joy. You told me to do it and I listened.

JoAnn, who always knew it would be easy to "know my fire" and had the patience to wait for the fire.

LET'S GRILL.

Contents

Grilling with
Chef George Hirsch

Introduction

I received my first "know your fire" lesson when I was about five or six years old. There were, I was taught, three kinds of wood you needed to build a fire: twigs for kindling, branches for getting the fire going, and heavier logs that become the charcoal.

My job was to collect the kindling, and I can remember bringing back an armful only to have my father or older sisters judge my efforts as unacceptable. Of course, I thought it was because I was the youngest in the family, but now I know they knew more about building a fire than I did. The wood I brought back was usually green.

Since then I've learned the techniques of building fires and how they work. When I had an understanding of what was happening with food in terms of the fire, I began to wonder why foods cooked in home kitchens and commercial restaurants couldn't be transferred to the outdoor grill.

My fascination with grilling became the genesis of the PBS series *Grilling with Chef George Hirsch* and the recipes demonstrated on the show have found their way into this book. And I've done these recipes over and over again at the American Bistro, my restaurant in Kings Park, Long Island, which opened in July 1989.

You'll find unexpected recipes for grilled pizzas, pastas, soups, sauces, vegetables, and desserts as well as for game, seafood, salads, beef, poultry, and lamb, and a whole section on smoking.

When you think of dishes you can prepare on the grill, most people don't put soups, salads, and pasta at the top of the list. But you can incorporate grilled vegetables, meats, seafood, and poultry into your soups and simmer the pot right on the grill. Again, grilled foods add a lot of flavor to salads. And, if you have a side burner on your grill, boiling the water for pasta while you grill the sauce ingredients keeps all the cooking out of doors.

One of the things I learned during many years at the grill was how the food you're using reacts to heat. Garlic, for instance, has a lot of innate sugars. When you know your fire, you learn that if you put garlic on a very high heat, it will burn on the outside and be hard on the inside. When cooking pork, fat will drip onto the fire and cause flare-ups, so it should be cooked over indirect heat.

My experience with cooking over an open fire began at an early age. Like most kids, it meant finding a stick, whittling down the end, and sticking on a hot dog or a marshmallow. Of course, the first few always fell into the fire.

Way back then, grills and equipment were not very high-tech. My parents were traditionalists. I remember how we would dig a pit, line it with rocks, and place a grate over it or fashion a spit by driving a couple of stakes into the ground. I never saw an actual grill until I was a teenager.

Even now, I find myself stretching my neck into people's backyards, curious about what types of grills they have and what's cooking. I've seen everything from half-barrels down in Georgia to grills dragged around the country on hitches attached to motor homes.

Wherever I go, it seems that everyone is intrigued by fire. Maybe it goes back to the time when cavemen used to bond around the open fire. I've noticed that the same thing happens around the grill. As soon as the fire is lit, people begin to gravitate to the grill to see what's going on.

Yet many people have a predetermined concept when it comes to grilling. They take a slab of meat, soak it in a secret marinade, and throw it on the grill. If you know your fire, you can have fun making pasta or cooking pizza on the grill. It doesn't have to be only burgers and hot dogs all year round. In the spring, grill the first asparagus and baby lamb while you're turning over the garden; in the fall, cook squash soup or *osso buco* while you're raking leaves. If you don't want to smoke a turkey because it takes six hours, smoke tuna. If your fishmonger doesn't have tuna, buy cod. So what if it's not usually smoked. Try it. Have fun. *Know your fire.*

Getting
Started

•••

Regardless of which type of grill you choose, always read the manufacturer's instructions carefully and keep them handy so that you can refer to them.

Charcoal Versus Gas Grilling

Grilling with gas is convenient. Gas grills are easy to light and cheap to operate, and they allow you to begin cooking almost immediately. On the other hand, these grills cost more than traditional charcoal grills and are usually fairly heavy. And, if you run out of propane, dinner will be late.

Charcoal is the traditional fuel for grills, but you have to wait for it to become embers before you start to cook. This means that you must plan ahead and light the charcoal about 45 minutes before you put the food on the grill. Charcoal grills are inexpensive, but you have to keep buying and storing charcoal, and you have to get rid of the ashes.

Kinds of Grills

Hibachi This small and inexpensive grill is seen on many fire escapes and terraces in big cities, and it's portable enough to carry along to the beach. The grill level is slightly adjustable, but the surface is only large enough for a few burgers or hot dogs, a small chicken, or a piece of fish.

Mobile Brazier In the fifties, when everyone moved to the suburbs and had a backyard, one of the things first-time homeowners purchased after the storm windows and the lawn mower was a brazier-style barbecue. It was a basic firebox that stood on three legs, two of which had wheels, making it portable. When you tried to outdo your neighbor, you bought the model with the hood, rotisserie, and air vents. Removing ashes was (and still is) a messy job.

Kettle-type Grill This very popular grill looks like a large two-piece ball with a handle on top. It sits on three legs and comes in many different sizes. Unfortunately, the grill surface is stationary, and you regulate the fire by opening and closing the air vents. You can cook steak on the grill, or a turkey with the cover on. There's a hole in the bottom for removing ashes.

Wagon-type Grill This is a large, heavy grill fueled by either gas, hardwood, or charcoal. It usually has at least one shelf on the side or underneath, and some have side burners in which you can boil a pot of water, sauté an onion, or perk a pot of coffee. Although these grills can be expensive, they last a long time, and replacement parts are readily available. If you cook with gas in the kitchen, you can connect a gas grill right into the main gas line. The charcoal model comes with a door on the front for adding hardwood or charcoal.

Indoor Grill Many new or renovated houses have an electric grill installed in the kitchen. Some are drop-in units that fit into the space of two stovetop burners. More elaborate versions are built into tile or brick walls.

Tuscan Fireplace Grill This is a portable grid that can be raised or lowered. It is fastened to an upright pole and fits into your fireplace.

Smoker Available in gas, electric, and charcoal models, the smoker is built on three levels: The heat source is on the bottom, the food is on the top, and there's a pan of water in the center. Wet wood chips are placed on the heat; they create flavored smoke that permeates the food.

Grill Pan This is a seasoned cast-iron stovetop pan with raised ridges that make grill marks on meat and vegetables. Any fat drops in between the ridges and can be poured off. Some new versions come with a nonstick surface.

Fuels for the Fire

Briquets are the traditional square black chunks of charcoal. They're cheap and are sold in every supermarket and convenience store. Since they're made from sawdust and scrap wood rather than solid wood, they don't get as hot as other fuels, and you'll need to use more of them. Avoid those impregnated with starter fluid, because they can give an "off" taste to food. Store briquets in a tight container; if they get damp, they take longer to ignite. Light the fire about 45 minutes before you expect to begin cooking.

Hardwood Charcoal, made from oak and other hardwoods, burns hot and slow with a minimum of ash. It's fairly expensive, but the fire can be doused with water and the charcoal used again. It is sold mostly in hardware stores.

Mesquite Charcoal, made from mesquite wood, burns fast and clean and imparts a pleasant aroma to meats, fish, and poultry. Beware of sparks when the wood is lighted. Mesquite charcoal is fairly expensive and is sold at upscale hardware stores and gourmet shops. It can be reused.

A Wood Fire is cheap if the wood is free and readily available. It takes about an hour for a wood fire to get hot enough for grilling. Use only seasoned hardwoods like oak, alder, hickory, and mesquite and fruitwoods like apple and cherry. Avoid softwoods like pine, which contain a lot of pitch. Never use wood that has been painted or chemically treated.

Propane cooking is inexpensive and convenient. Turn on the heat and the grill is ready to go in a few minutes. There's even an accessory you can buy that indicates when the tank is getting low and it's time for a refill. Charcoal aficionados don't believe you get the smoky flavor associated with grilling when you use gas, but it's so easy to use that you may not even notice the difference. Hardwood charcoal briquets are available for certain types of propane grills; they give the convenience of gas with the flavor of the charcoal.

How to Light the Fire

Paper and Kindling are the tried-and-true materials for lighting any kind of fire, but they're not always effective, especially on a windy day. Here's the best method: Tightly crumble a few sheets of newspaper into a ball, lay some kindling on top in a pyramid fashion, and cover the kindling with briquets. When you light the paper, it will light the kindling and, hopefully, the briquets.

Electric Starters offer an easy way to light a fire, but you need an electric outlet close by or a long extension cord. Simple, reliable, and cheap, an electric starter is basically the element used in an electric stove with a handle attached. There is one drawback: Only the briquets touching the hot starter will ignite. Remove the starter after the briquets ignite; it will be very hot, so set it aside in a safe place.

A Metal Chimney is the quickest and safest way to light a fire. It resembles a large juice can with a handle on the side and air holes around the lower edge. You fill the chamber with crumbled paper on the bottom and charcoal on top. Once the paper is lit, the flame is drawn up into the charcoal area and ignites the charcoal. This should take from 10 to 15 minutes. You then walk over to the grill and dump the coals onto it.

Fire Sticks are small cubes or sticks made of sawdust and paraffin. You place one under a stack of charcoal and light it. They work well but are expensive. You can make your own by mixing melted paraffin with sawdust and pouring the mixture into a cardboard egg box. When the mixture hardens, cut apart the individual segments.

Lighter Fluid works very well, but it has caused flashbacks that have resulted in terrible accidents. In some states, it is even illegal to use it, so avoid it like the plague.

Indirect Versus Direct Cooking on the Grill

Direct Cooking means just that: cooking food directly over a hot fire for a period of less than 25 minutes.

Indirect Grilling means pushing the coals aside and placing a pan in the center to catch drippings. This is especially useful when cooking fatty foods such as pork or large roasts and turkeys. It can also mean cooking with the hood lowered. The internal temperature rises, the air gets hot, and the food is more roasted than grilled.

Flavoring the Smoke

Most kinds of aromatic wood or wood chips, such as hickory, mesquite, apple, and vine cuttings, can be soaked in water and placed on a charcoal fire. On a gas grill, however, you want to prevent ashes from clogging the line, so place the chips in a disposable aluminum pan and poke some holes in the bottom, or purchase a smoker box.

When Is the Fire Ready for Cooking?

Before you light a charcoal fire, you have to know how much charcoal to use. Imagine how much room your food will take up on the grill. Use enough charcoal to make a single layer below that space, and throw in a few more briquets.

As a general rule, it takes about 45 minutes for charcoal to get hot enough for grilling. When the coals are covered with a gray ash, spread them into a single layer. Arrange the briquets closer together in the center so the fire will be hotter there, and leave some space between the coals on the edges for a cooler fire.

Hold your hand, palm side down, 5 inches over the fire. If your hand gets hot immediately, the fire is very hot. If you can hold it there for 2 to 3 seconds, the fire is hot; 4 to 5 seconds, the fire is medium; and 6 seconds, the fire is low.

Is It Done Yet?

Grilling is an art; there are no strict rules. Cooking time will depend on the temperature of the food as well as the temperature of the fire and the air. If the wind is blowing or the humidity is high, food takes longer to cook. The only way to tell for sure is to use an instant-read thermometer and start checking when fish becomes opaque, the juices in chicken run clear, and meat gets a crusty finish.

How to Put Out the Fire

Putting out a gas fire is as simple as turning the knob to "off" and closing the valve on the gas tank. On a charcoal grill with a lid, close the air vents and replace the cover. On an open grill, pour some water on the coals or wood and check in 30 minutes to see if the fire is indeed out.

Cleaning the Grill

Although it's not everyone's favorite job, occasionally someone has to clean the grill. A clean grate cooks better and the food doesn't stick. Remove any food from the cooking grate with a stiff wire brush or a wad of aluminum foil. If you have a charcoal grill, remove the ashes frequently. Once a year, spray porcelain surfaces with oven cleaner and wipe with paper towel.

To clean the grate on a gas grill, turn the grill on "high," close the lid, and wait 10 to 15 minutes. Scrape off any residue with a stiff brush or a wad of aluminum foil. Wipe out the interior frequently to remove grease.

Tools of the Trade

Heavy-duty, Long-handled, Spring-loaded Tongs Never turn a piece of meat with a fork. The tines will break the surface and release the juices. Instead, use spring-loaded tongs.

Offset Spatula A spatula with a 7-inch blade comes in handy when turning a fish fillet or a hamburger.

Basting Brush A long-handled one is perfect when you have to baste food while it's cooking.

Bamboo or Metal Skewers Skewers should be flat so that the food doesn't rotate as it's being turned. Bamboo skewers should be soaked in water for 30 minutes before being used on the grill so they don't burn. Because bamboo skewers make a smaller hole, they usually keep food from turning, but if this should happen, use two skewers about ½ inch apart.

Heavy-duty, Long-handled Wire Brush Use this for cleaning the grill. It works best when the grill is hot.

Instant-read Meat Thermometer This comes in handy when you're cooking a large piece of meat such as a roast or a turkey. Remember, the food will continue to cook after it has been removed from the grill, so take it off when the thermometer registers 5°F. less than you want.

Heavy-duty Grill Mitts The heat from a grill can get very intense. Use mitts, not a cloth or apron, when touching anything hot.

Hinged Grill Baskets These hold foods that are small or difficult to turn, such as fish, shrimp, burgers, and vegetables.

Porcelain Grilling Racks are screens with small holes that fit over the grate and prevent delicate foods from falling into the fire.

A Spray Bottle filled with water is handy to keep around in case of flare-ups. Some outdoor grillers use water pistols instead.

A Smoker Box can turn a regular charcoal or propane grill into a smoker. It's a 4 by 6-inch box made of a heavy metal, such as iron. Soaked wood chips are placed in the smoker box. As they heat, they create smoke and flavor the food. The smoker box holds the ashes from the chips and keeps the grill clean.

Health Concerns

Although you may have heard about health risks resulting from foods cooked over extremely high heats, or that smoked foods contain life-threatening carcinogens, no scientific study to date has proved that grilling poses health hazards.

It's true that fat dripping onto hot coals can flare up and create minute amounts of harmful substances, but they are so infinitesimal that they do not pose a problem.

Older gas grills had lava rocks that caught the grease and caused flare-ups. In newer models, fat falls onto metal bars and evaporates.

If you're still concerned, place a drip pan below the meat to catch drippings before they reach the hot coals, and use the indirect method of grilling—that is, grilling with the top down. Or parcook meat such as chicken or pork by simmering it in water on a stovetop or cooking it in the microwave oven to remove most of the fat before placing it on the grill.

The real danger in grilling comes from the improper handling of food. If it's taking longer than expected to get the fire going, make sure all meat, fish, and poultry is refrigerated and not left out in the hot sun.

And remember that grilled meats usually have less fat than meats cooked by other methods, because no fat is added for cooking.

Appetizers

The purpose of appetizers is to wake up the taste buds. They set the stage for the rest of the meal and should be chosen carefully. Appetizers should look delicious, smell marvelous, and taste even better. When feeding a crowd, choose different textures and colors and vary the flavors. If you're serving chicken as the main course, don't choose chicken wings as an appetizer. Many appetizers are finger foods, so have plenty of napkins around.

Bruschetta

Something wonderful happens to country-style bread when it's brushed with olive oil and grilled. Its smoky flavor is the perfect foil for fresh tomatoes seasoned with lots of caramelized garlic, Parmesan cheese, and capers. Day-old bread makes the best bruschetta, so this is a good way to use up yesterday's loaf of Italian, French, or sourdough bread. Serve bruschetta with salad or soup, or as a snack with a chunk of pepperoni.

3 cups seeded and diced plum tomatoes

24 cloves Caramelized Garlic (page 111)

2 tablespoons grated Parmesan cheese

1 tablespoon capers, rinsed

Salt and pepper to taste

12 slices round country-style bread, sliced ¾ inch thick

¼ cup olive oil

6 basil leaves, chopped

Grated Parmesan cheese

To make the topping, combine the tomatoes, garlic, Parmesan cheese, capers, salt, and pepper.

Brush the bread on both sides with olive oil and grill for 10 to 15 seconds on each side. Press down on the bread with a spatula so that the bread picks up grill marks.

When the bread is grilled, top the slices evenly with the tomato mixture and place them in a foil pan on the grill. Close the hood and heat for 4 to 5 minutes. Remove the pan and sprinkle each bruschetta with basil and Parmesan cheese.

Smoked Pecans

Makes 6 servings

Toss the pecans with a mild-flavored olive oil and save the extra-virgin olive oil for salads. Try apple or cherry wood in the smoker for mild-flavored nuts or mesquite for a more robust flavor. Serve these as a snack with drinks or sprinkle a few on soups, salads, pastas, or pizzas.

2 teaspoons olive oil

2 teaspoons butter, melted

1 pound pecan halves

Sea salt to taste

Prepare a smoker.

Using a small wooden skewer, poke a hole in the bottom of a 9- by 7-inch heavy-duty, disposable aluminum-foil pan. Combine the olive oil, butter, and pecans in the pan and toss well. Place the pan on the top rack of the smoker and smoke for 1 hour, stirring the nuts every 20 minutes.

Frittata

Makes 4 to 6 servings

**Grill
temperature**

**high,
then medium**

A frittata is like a quiche, but it doesn't have a crust, which makes it lower in calories. Mix in some chopped prosciutto or salami, shredded Cheddar cheese, or precooked seafood or chicken, and it becomes an entree for lunch or brunch. When made with spinach or mushrooms, a frittata can be a served as a side-dish vegetable. For low-cholesterol diets, use ¼ cup or 2 ounces of egg substitute for each egg.

½ cup filling (cooked vegetable, seafood, meat, cheese, etc.)

10 eggs, well beaten

¼ cup half-and-half

2 tablespoons grated Parmesan cheese

¼ teaspoon Tabasco sauce

⅛ teaspoon ground nutmeg

Salt and pepper to taste

Place the filling in a buttered 10-inch metal pie pan or skillet. Beat the eggs with the half-and-half, Parmesan cheese, Tabasco, nutmeg, salt, and pepper. Pour over the filling and place the pan over high heat on the grill. Stir the egg mixture. When the eggs begin to set, lower the hood and cook on medium for 4 to 5 minutes, or until firm yet moist.

Portobello Mushrooms
with Belgian Endive

Makes 2 luncheon servings or 4 appetizer servings

Portobello mushrooms are the largest of all the cultivated mushrooms, with caps often reaching 6 to 7 inches across. They're so meaty, eating one is almost like cutting into a piece of steak. Other bitter greens, such as escarole or chicory, can be used instead of endive.

4 Portobello mushrooms

¼ cup olive oil

2 lemons, sliced thin

4 heads Belgian endive

Freshly ground black pepper to taste

Cut the stems from the mushrooms and save them for stock or sauce. Wipe the caps with a dampened paper towel. (Or rinse them quickly under water and pat dry if they're very dirty.) Brush both sides of the mushrooms with some of the olive oil. Place the mushrooms on the grill, gill sides up, and cook for 4 to 5 minutes. Turn the mushrooms over, placing them on the cooler edges of the grill, and cook for 6 to 8 minutes, or until tender. At the same time, grill the lemon slices.

Separate the leaves of the endive and arrange them on four serving dishes. Place a mushroom, gill side down, in the center of each dish, and top with grilled lemon slices. Drizzle with the remaining olive oil and sprinkle with pepper.

Grill temperature

medium-high, then low

Grilled Marinated Peppers

Makes 4 to 6 servings

Grilled marinated peppers are one of those versatile vegetables you can store in the refrigerator for several days and use in a variety of ways. Dress them up with Caramelized Garlic and a few leaves of chopped basil, or layer them with slices of fresh mozzarella and vine-ripened tomatoes. Make the world's fastest pasta sauce by combining chopped marinated peppers with a little extra olive oil, a dash of red pepper flakes, and some grated Parmesan cheese. And make the world's easiest low-calorie sauce by pureeing the peppers and serving the puree over meats and seafood.

6 large, firm red bell peppers

½ cup olive oil

Wash the peppers and place them on the grill over high heat. Turn them over several times, and move them to medium heat once they begin to char. (The total cooking time should be 15 to 20 minutes.) Once they're black all over, remove them from the heat, immediately place them in a large bowl, and cover with plastic wrap. Leave them there until they cool and the skins separate from the flesh. Remove the peppers, run them under cold water, and peel off the skins. Slice the peppers in half, and remove and discard the seeds and ribs. Dry the peppers and cover them with olive oil.

Sweet Potato Home-Fries

Makes 4 servings

As the natural sugars in sweet potatoes and onions caramelize on the grill, the flavor of each vegetable improves, resulting in a dish that is greater than the sum of its parts.

We began serving these home-fries at the restaurant as a side dish with steak, but they became so popular we put them on the menu as an appetizer.

4 large sweet potatoes

2 onions, sliced thin

4 tablespoons (½ stick) butter

¼ teaspoon ground nutmeg

Salt and pepper to taste

Wash the sweet potatoes and wrap them in heavy-duty aluminum foil. Place them on the grill for 30 to 40 minutes, depending on their size, turning them occasionally. Remove them when they're still a bit firm when pierced with a sharp knife. Allow them to cool. Unwrap the potatoes and discard the foil. Peel the potatoes and cut them into ¼-inch slices.

Place the sweet potatoes in a large nonstick skillet or a black cast-iron skillet and add the onion, butter, nutmeg, salt, and pepper. Place on high heat and cook, stirring frequently, until the potatoes are tender and slightly brown.

Grill temperature

medium-high, then high

19

Appetizers

Quesadillas

Quesadillas are sort of like Southwestern-style pizzas. Their intense flavors make them great appetizers as well as great party foods, and the fillings are good ways to use up leftovers.

Brush one side of a tortilla with olive oil. Turn the tortilla over and spread the desired filling on one half of the tortilla.

Fold the plain side over the filling and press firmly. Place the tortilla on the grill over low heat. Cook for 4 to 5 minutes on each side, then move to medium heat and allow the tortilla to crisp up. Remove the quesadilla from the grill and cut it into four wedges.

Black Bean with
Jack and Blue Quesadilla

Makes 8 to 10 appetizer servings

Grill
temperature

medium

Gorgonzola cheese adds a bit of zip to the filling.

½ cup shredded Monterey Jack cheese

½ cup crumbled Gorgonzola cheese

¼ cup diced tomato

One 16-ounce can black beans, rinsed and drained

1 tablespoon chopped cilantro

¼ cup olive oil

6 flour tortillas

Salsa (page 25)

In a medium bowl, combine all of the ingredients except the tortillas and mix well. Spread the mixture on the tortillas and follow the quesadilla grilling instructions on page 20. Serve with salsa.

Grilled Chicken with Peppers Quesadilla

Makes 8 to 10 appetizer servings

Grill temperature

medium, then high

Monterey Jack cheese is a mild Cheddar-type cheese that originated in Monterey, California. It is named after David Jacks, who first made the cheese during the gold-rush years.

> 1 whole chicken breast, skinless, boneless
>
> Olive oil
>
> 2 red bell peppers
>
> 1 cup shredded Monterey Jack cheese
>
> ¼ cup olive oil
>
> 2 tablespoons chopped scallion
>
> 1 tablespoon chopped cilantro
>
> 6 flour tortillas
>
> Salsa (page 25)

Brush the chicken breast with olive oil and grill for 4 to 5 minutes on each side, or until no longer pink in the center. Cool slightly and slice thin. Brush the peppers with oil and grill them over high heat, turning frequently, until charred. Remove from the grill, peel off the skins, remove the seeds, and chop coarsely.

In a medium bowl, combine the chicken slices, chopped roasted peppers, cheese, ¼ cup olive oil, scallion, and cilantro, and mix well. Spread the mixture on the tortillas and follow the quesadilla grilling instructions on page 20. Serve with salsa.

Shrimp with Mozzarella Quesadilla

Makes 8 to 10 appetizer servings

Twelve cloves of caramelized garlic may seem like a lot, but they make this filling extra good.

Grill
temperature

medium

1 pound medium shrimp (26 to 30 per pound), peeled and deveined

1 cup shredded mozzarella

12 cloves Caramelized Garlic (page 111)

2 tablespoons grated Parmesan cheese

¼ cup chopped red bell pepper

¼ cup olive oil

6 basil leaves, chopped

6 flour tortillas

Salsa (page 25)

Thread the shrimp on skewers and grill for 4 to 5 minutes on each side. Remove the shrimp from the grill and, when they cool slightly, cut them into small pieces. In a medium bowl, combine the shrimp with the remaining ingredients, except the tortillas, and mix well. Spread the mixture on the tortillas and follow the quesadilla grilling instructions on page 20. Serve with salsa.

Trio of Cheeses with Smoked Pecans and Grilled Onion Quesadilla

Makes 8 to 10 appetizer servings

Three cheeses are always better than one, and the smoked pecans set off their flavors.

1 large onion

1 cup Smoked Pecans (page 15)

⅓ cup shredded Monterey Jack cheese

⅓ cup shredded mozzarella

⅓ cup shredded Cheddar cheese

¼ cup olive oil

1 tablespoon chopped cilantro

6 flour tortillas

Salsa (page 25)

Cut the onion horizontally into thick slices and grill them for 5 minutes on each side. When the onion cools slightly, chop it coarsely.

In a medium bowl, combine the chopped grilled onion, pecans, cheeses, olive oil, and cilantro, and mix well. Spread the mixture on the tortillas and follow the quesadilla grilling instructions on page 20. Serve with salsa.

Salsa

Makes about 3 cups

Roasting the tomatoes first gives the salsa a wonderful smoky flavor

Grill
temperature

high

8 to 10 plum tomatoes

1 red onion

Juice of 2 limes

2 jalapeño peppers, chopped (optional)

½ cup peeled, seeded, and diced cucumber

¼ teaspoon Tabasco sauce

2 tablespoons chopped cilantro

Salt and pepper to taste

Place the tomatoes on the grill and cook, turning several times, until they are slightly charred. Cool slightly and chop coarsely. Slice the onion and grill for 2 to 3 minutes on each side. Cool slightly and chop coarsely.

In a medium bowl, combine the tomato with the remaining ingredients. Mix well and set aside for 1 hour to allow the flavors to develop.

Grilled Vegetables
with Guacamole

The avocados must be properly ripe, and they'll never achieve their full taste potential if they're refrigerated. Remember: the best avocados are shipped ripe and are not allowed to ripen on the produce counter.

2 large onions

1 eggplant

2 red bell peppers

2 green bell peppers

¼ cup olive oil

Juice and zest of 1 lime

1 teaspoon ground cumin

½ teaspoon coriander

Freshly ground black pepper to taste

1 recipe Guacamole (recipe follows)

Cut the onion, eggplant, and peppers into ¼-inch slices. In a large nonreactive bowl, combine the olive oil, lime juice and zest, cumin, coriander, and black pepper. Place the vegetables in the marinade, toss gently, and set aside for 1 hour at room temperature. Remove the vegetables from the marinade and grill for 3 to 4 minutes on each side. Serve with guacamole and warm grilled tortillas.

Guacamole

Makes 4 to 6 servings

Never make guacamole far in advance because avocados discolor very quickly when exposed to air. Some people use only a stainless-steel knife to cut the avocados, and others stick the pit in the center of the guacamole to prevent darkening. I suggest eating it fast.

> **3 to 4 large, ripe avocados**
>
> **1 large tomato, diced**
>
> **5 cloves Caramelized Garlic (page 111)**
>
> **Juice of 1 lime**
>
> **2 tablespoons chopped cilantro**
>
> **½ teaspoon red pepper flakes**
>
> **Salt and pepper to taste**

Peel the avocados, discard the pits, and remove any bad spots. Cut them into ½-inch dice. In a medium nonreactive bowl, combine the avocado with the remaining ingredients. Mix well, cover the dish, and refrigerate for 1 hour.

Smaking Wings

Makes 32 pieces

Grill temperature

medium-high

Smaking wings are a tangy and sweet version of Buffalo wings, a festive dish that is perfect for parties. To increase the "sweat quotient," add more pepper and Tabasco.

A chicken wing has three parts. Remove the bony wing tips and save them for stock. Cut the other two pieces apart. The center section with the double bone can be made into "lollipops": Simply cut the tendon at the knob end of the wing and slide the meat down. This gives you a bone with a chunk of meat or "lollipop" at the end.

16 chicken wings

½ cup salad oil

¼ cup balsamic vinegar

¼ cup honey

2 tablespoons brown sugar

2 tablespoons cane syrup or dark corn syrup

1 tablespoon Tabasco sauce

½ teaspoon red pepper flakes

½ teaspoon dried thyme

1 teaspoon soy sauce

¼ teaspoon Worcestershire sauce

¼ teaspoon cayenne

¼ teaspoon ground nutmeg

Grilling
with
Chef
George
Hirsch

Cut off and discard the bony wing tips. Cut the remaining wings in half.

In a large bowl, combine the remaining ingredients and mix well. Marinate the wings in this mixture for 1 hour in the refrigerator, then grill for 15 to 20 minutes, turning frequently.

Chicken Liver Brochette

Makes 4 to 6 appetizer servings

Chicken livers are not on the top of everyone's priority list, but the teriyaki marinade makes them very flavorful and removes any bitter taste they may have. If you use bamboo skewers, soak them in water for about 30 minutes so they won't burn on the grill. They make a nice presentation with the pineapple.

Grill temperature

medium

> ½ **pound bacon, cut into 2-inch pieces**
>
> I **pound chicken livers, trimmed and split**
>
> **4 to 6 bamboo skewers**
>
> ½ **cup sliced water chestnuts**
>
> I **cup canned pineapple chunks**
>
> I **recipe Teriyaki Marinade (page I50)**

Wrap the bacon pieces around the chicken livers and arrange them on the skewers, alternating with the water chestnuts and pineapple chunks. Place the skewers in the marinade for 30 minutes. Remove and grill for 12 to 15 minutes, basting frequently. Be careful not to overcook the livers; they should be slightly pink inside.

Grilled Tortilla Chips

Makes 6 to 8 servings

These tortilla chips are delicious by themselves or with dips. Use white-flour or soft yellow-corn tortillas.

¼ **cup grated Parmesan cheese**

I **teaspoon salt**

¼ **teaspoon ground cumin**

¼ **teaspoon paprika**

¼ **teaspoon coriander**

¼ **teaspoon cayenne**

Eight to ten 10-inch flour or corn tortillas

¼ **cup olive oil**

In a small bowl, combine the Parmesan cheese, salt, cumin, paprika, coriander, and cayenne, and mix well.

Brush the tortillas lightly on both sides with olive oil and place them on the grill for approximately 30 to 45 seconds. As soon as the tortillas begin to blister, turn them and grill 30 seconds longer. Remove immediately and sprinkle with seasoning.

Soups

●●●

If you want to make great soups, you have to start out with great ingredients, and not just any leftovers you have in the refrigerator. Soup is versatile. On a warm summer's night, a rich seafood soup can be the whole meal, while a chilled soup would go well with grilled meat or seafood.

Chicken Stock

Makes I quart

Grill temperature

high, then low

Stock is the foundation of all good soups and sauces. It is very simple (though time-consuming) to make and can be prepared in advance. Collect bones, wings, necks, and backs from chickens and freeze them until you have enough. (A true stock is made with bones, as compared to a bouillon, which uses just the meat.) Once the stock is chilled, remove any yellow fat that congeals on top.

2½ to 3 pounds chicken bones, carcass, or backs and necks

I large onion, chopped

2 carrots, chopped

2 ribs celery, chopped

2 bay leaves

4 to 5 parsley stems

¼ teaspoon dried thyme or 4 to 5 fresh sprigs

4 cloves garlic, chopped

7 cups water

Combine all of the ingredients in a 1-gallon stockpot and bring to a boil on the grill or stovetop. Reduce the heat and simmer for 1½ hours. Skim off any surface fat and strain the stock, discarding the solids. Cool and refrigerate for 2 to 3 days, or freeze for up to 2 months.

Fish Stock

Makes I quart

When making fish stock, be careful not to toss in any celery leaves or onion peelings, as they can make the stock bitter. The stock should cook for no more than 20 to 25 minutes.

Grill temperature

high, then low

I tablespoon olive oil

I large leek, white part only, cleaned and chopped

I onion, chopped

I rib celery, chopped

I parsnip, chopped

I pound fish bones (flounder, halibut, cod) or shellfish shells
(shrimp, lobster)

I cup white wine

2 bay leaves

4 stems fresh parsley

4 stems fresh thyme

5 cups water

Heat the olive oil in a 2-quart stockpot on the grill or stove top. Add the leek, onion, celery, and parsnip, and sauté, taking care not to allow the vegetables to color. Add the fish bones or shells, wine, bay leaves, parsley, thyme, and water. Bring to a boil, lower the heat, and simmer for 25 to 30 minutes. Strain and discard the vegetables and bones. Cool the stock and refrigerate for up to 2 days, or freeze for up to 2 weeks.

Vegetable Stock

Makes I quart

Vegetable stock is good to use with nonmeat pasta sauces and other vegetarian dishes. Brown the vegetables first on the grill or in a stockpot; they will give off more flavor after they have caramelized. For even more taste, add chopped ears of fresh corn or sweet potatoes.

> **2 tablespoons olive oil**
>
> **2 large onions, chopped fine**
>
> **3 ribs celery, chopped fine**
>
> **3 carrots, chopped fine**
>
> **2 parsnips, chopped fine**
>
> **2 white turnips, chopped fine**
>
> **2 tomatoes, chopped fine**
>
> **3 bay leaves**
>
> **4 to 6 stems fresh parsley**
>
> **½ teaspoon dried thyme**
>
> **4 cloves garlic, chopped**
>
> **7 cups water**

In a large stockpot on a grill or stovetop, heat the olive oil. Add the onion, celery, and carrot, and sauté until the vegetables turn light brown. (If you cook the vegetables longer, the stock will be darker in color.) Add the parsnip, turnip, tomato, bay leaves, parsley, thyme, garlic, and water. (Or grill the vegetables whole before adding them to the stockpot.) Bring to a boil, lower the heat, and simmer gently for 1½ to 2 hours. Strain and discard the vegetables. Cool the broth and refrigerate for up to 4 days, or freeze for up to 2 months.

Shinnecock
Clam Chowder

Makes 6 servings

This is an authentic Indian-style recipe. Unlike most chowders, which call for chopping the clams, this version uses them whole. To really enjoy this chowder, eat it out of doors.

¼ pound salt pork, chopped fine

2 large onions, diced

4 medium potatoes, peeled and diced

4 cups fish stock

2 dozen chowder clams or quahogs, well scrubbed

2 tablespoons chopped fresh Italian parsley

Salt and pepper to taste

Cook the salt pork over the grill or stovetop in a 1-gallon stockpot until it gives up all its fat. Add the onion and cook until it begins to turn light brown. Add the potato and stock and cook for 10 to 15 minutes, or until the potato is tender. Add the clams and cook for 3 to 4 minutes or until shells open. Stir in the parsley and season with salt and pepper.

Grill
temperature

Corn-Seafood Chowder

Makes 4 to 6 luncheon or first-course dinner servings

Grilling the fish and vegetables first imparts a wonderful smoky flavor to this clam-and-cod chowder. The optional heavy cream makes the soup smooth and flavorful, but if you can't afford the calories, substitute an equal amount of half-and-half and it will be almost as good. Serve the chowder with grilled bruschetta.

Eight 10-ounce cod fillets or other firm white flaky fish

Olive oil

½ onion, cut into ½-inch slices

4 scallions

½ green bell pepper, cut in half

3 ears fresh corn or one 10-ounce can corn niblets

6 chowder clams, shucked and chopped, or one 7-ounce can
    chopped clams

1 head Caramelized Garlic (page 111)

2 cups clam juice or fish bouillon

1 cup unpeeled diced red new potato

1 teaspoon Tabasco sauce, or to taste

1 teaspoon dried thyme

1 teaspoon dried rosemary, crumbled

Sea salt to taste

1 cup heavy cream or half-and-half

Brush the cod fillets with olive oil and grill them for 3 minutes on each side. Brush the onion, scallions, and bell pepper with olive oil and grill for 3 minutes on each side. Cool the vegetables slightly and dice.

Place the vegetables and fish in a large stockpot on the side burner of the grill or on a stovetop. Using a sharp knife, cut the kernels from the corn and place them in the pot along with the clams, caramelized garlic, clam juice, potato, Tabasco, thyme, rosemary, and salt. Bring to a simmer and cook for 4 to 5 minutes or until potato is tender. Add the cream and cook for 1 to 2 minutes. Serve with bruschetta.

Oyster Stew

Makes 4 servings

**Grill
temperature**

**high,
then low**

Oyster stew is a very popular dish at seafood restaurants in Manhattan. But no matter how good it may be, it can be a disaster if it contains any sand—so don't skip the strain-the-shucking-liquid step. Never overcook the oysters or they will taste like rocks.

2 cups shucked oysters with accumulated juices

¼ teaspoon sweet paprika

¼ teaspoon dry mustard

¼ teaspoon dried parsley

¼ teaspoon Tabasco sauce

¼ teaspoon Worcestershire sauce

2 tablespoons butter

4 cups half-and-half

Salt and ground white pepper to taste

Oyster crackers or toast points

Strain the shucked oysters, reserving the juices. Place the oyster liquid in a medium stockpot on the grill or stovetop, add the paprika, mustard, parsley, Tabasco and Worcestershire sauce, and bring to a rolling boil. Add the oysters and simmer for 2 to 3 minutes, or until the edges of the oysters curl. Add the butter and half-and-half and cook for 1 minute. Season with salt and white pepper. Serve immediately with oyster crackers or toast points.

Potato-Leek Soup

Makes 6 servings

If you've always eaten potato-leek soup cold, try this one on a hot summer's eve and see what you think. Use either boiling potatoes or russets, not new or bliss potatoes which will make the soup gummy.

The recipe calls for pureeing two thirds of the soup, but this step can be omitted. This is a very flavorful and earthy dish that is especially good in the fall. Grilling the onion and leek before cutting them will improve their taste.

2 tablespoons butter

I cup diced onion

I cup washed and chopped leek, white part only

2 cloves garlic, chopped

I tablespoon all-purpose flour

4 cups peeled and diced potato

2 quarts chicken or vegetable stock

2 bay leaves

¼ teaspoon ground nutmeg

¼ teaspoon Tabasco sauce

2 cups heavy cream or half-and-half

Salt and pepper to taste

2 tablespoons snipped chives

In a 1-gallon stockpot on the grill or stovetop, heat the butter. Add the onion, leek, and garlic. Sauté for a minute or two, but do not allow the vegetables to color. Add the flour and mix well. Add the potato, stock, bay leaves, nutmeg, and Tabasco. Bring to a boil, lower the heat, and simmer for 45 minutes. Remove the bay leaves. Puree two thirds of the mixture in a food processor or blender. Return the puree to the pot and add the cream; simmer for 2 to 3 minutes. Season with salt and pepper. Sprinkle with chives.

Chicken-Corn Soup

Makes 6 servings

This soup is a good way to use corn when it looks so good you can't resist buying too much of it. Its origin is a Pennsylvania Dutch chicken soup with dumplings called knepp, where hard-cooked eggs are added at the last minute. Grilling the chicken before putting it in the pot is optional.

One 3-pound stewing chicken, cut into pieces

8 cups chicken stock

1 onion, chopped

½ cup chopped celery

½ cup chopped carrot

2 bay leaves

¼ teaspoon dried thyme

¼ teaspoon dried parsley

**3 cups kernels from Montauk Indian Corn on the Cob (page 112), or
two 12-ounce cans corn niblets, drained**

Grill
temperature

high,
then low

40

Grilling
with
Chef
George
Hirsch

Knepp

1 cup all-purpose flour

1 egg

½ teaspoon baking powder

3 hard-cooked eggs, chopped coarse

¼ teaspoon Tabasco sauce

Salt and pepper to taste

Place the chicken parts in a large stockpot on the grill or stovetop and add the stock, onion, celery, carrot, bay leaves, thyme, and parsley. Bring to a boil, lower the heat, and simmer for 45 minutes, or until the chicken is tender. Remove the chicken, and when it has cooled, remove the meat from the bones. Discard the bones and cut the chicken into bite-size pieces. Return the meat to the soup along with the corn kernels. Simmer for 15 minutes.

To make the knepp, combine the flour, egg, and baking powder in a medium bowl and mix together with a fork and knife until crumbly. Add small pieces of knepp to the soup, a few at a time. Cover and simmer gently for 10 minutes. Stir in the eggs and Tabasco. Remove the bay leaves and season with salt and pepper.

Five-Onion Soup

Makes 6 to 8 servings

**Grill
temperature**

**high,
then low**

I don't remember how we came up with this soup, but it had exceptional appeal in my restaurant, the American Bistro. It's really a bonus soup because it actually contains six, not five, onions if you count garlic as a family member. Don't stir this too often because you want the onions to caramelize. Quickly grill the onions before you slice them.

2 tablespoons butter

I cup finely sliced Spanish onion

I cup finely sliced red onion

I cup finely sliced leek, white part only

½ cup finely chopped shallot

I cup finely chopped scallion

6 cloves garlic, minced

2 tablespoons all-purpose flour

½ cup dry white wine

2 quarts chicken stock

2 bay leaves

¼ teaspoon Tabasco sauce

Salt and pepper to taste

Heat a 1-gallon stockpot on the grill or stovetop, and melt the butter. Add the Spanish onion, red onion, leek, shallot, scallion, and garlic, and cook, stirring occasionally, until the vegetables are browned but not burned. Stir in the flour and cook for 1 minute. Add the wine, chicken stock, bay leaves, and Tabasco. Bring to a boil, lower the temperature, and simmer for 35 to 40 minutes, skimming off any fat that rises to the surface. Remove the bay leaves and season with salt and pepper.

Gazpacho with Ceviche of Scallops

Makes 4 servings

Gazpacho doesn't require any cooking and, to carry the theme even further, the soup is dressed with a ceviche of scallops—shellfish "cooked" in lime juice. Marinating the vegetables in the tomato juice marries the flavors and improves the taste. Shrimp can be used instead of scallops.

½ **cup finely chopped onion**

4 **cups tomato juice**

Juice of I lemon

¼ **cup finely chopped red bell pepper**

¼ **cup finely chopped green bell pepper**

4 **cloves garlic, chopped fine**

¼ **cup finely chopped scallion**

½ **cup peeled, seeded, finely chopped cucumber**

I **tablespoon chopped cilantro**

¼ **teaspoon Tabasco sauce**

¼ **teaspoon Worcestershire sauce**

¼ **teaspoon ground cumin**

Ceviche

8 **ounces bay scallops**

Juice and zest of I lime

¼ cup tequila

¼ teaspoon red pepper flakes

½ tablespoon chopped cilantro

Tortilla Toast (page 58)

Place the onion in a small strainer and run under hot water. Squeeze tightly to remove liquid. In a large nonreactive bowl, combine the onion, tomato juice, lemon juice, red pepper, green pepper, garlic, scallion, cucumber, cilantro, Tabasco, Worcestershire sauce, and cumin. Mix well and chill for 2 hours.

In a medium bowl, combine the scallops, lime juice and zest, tequila, red pepper flakes, and cilantro, and toss gently. Marinate for 2 hours in the refrigerator. Add 2 to 3 tablespoons of ceviche to each serving of soup. Serve with Tortilla Toast.

Grilled Shrimp and Okra Gumbo

Makes 6 servings

Gumbo is a hearty soup found in Cajun cuisine and it always contains okra. In fact, the word *gumbo* comes from the African word *gombo*, which means "okra." In the Northeast, okra is not used very much, but in the Southeast it's very popular. In this recipe, marinated shrimp are grilled, removed from the skewers, and laid on top of the gumbo, rather than the more traditional method of cooking the raw shrimp in the soup.

1 pound medium shrimp (26 to 30 per pound), peeled and deveined

½ cup cane syrup or dark corn syrup

2 cloves garlic, chopped

½ teaspoon Tabasco sauce

½ teaspoon paprika

½ teaspoon dried basil

¼ teaspoon ground nutmeg

¼ teaspoon Worcestershire sauce

¼ cup vegetable oil

Gumbo

½ cup vegetable oil

¾ cup all-purpose flour

2½ cups sliced okra

1 cup sliced onion

½ cup chopped celery

½ cup chopped red bell pepper

6 cloves garlic, chopped fine

1 cup chopped scallion

6 cups fish stock

½ teaspoon Tabasco sauce

1 tablespoon filé powder, dissolved in 2 tablespoons water

Salt and pepper to taste

Place 5 to 6 shrimp on each skewer. Combine the cane syrup, garlic, Tabasco, paprika, basil, nutmeg, Worcestershire sauce, and vegetable oil in a shallow bowl. Add the shrimp and marinate in the refrigerator for 30 minutes. Grill for 7 to 8 minutes on medium-high and remove the skewers.

Heat the salad oil in a 1-gallon stockpot on the grill. Add the flour and cook slowly for 15 to 20 minutes, stirring constantly, until the mixture is light chocolate brown in color. Add the okra, onion, celery, red pepper, garlic, and scallion, and sauté for 3 to 5 minutes. Slowly whisk in the fish stock. Bring to a boil, lower the heat, and simmer for 25 to 30 minutes. Slowly stir in the filé powder–water mixture. Lay the marinated shrimp on top. Season with salt and pepper.

Crab Boil

Makes 4 servings

Crab boil is party food, and you should eat it in clothes that can move right into the washing machine. Ideally, this recipe should be prepared and served out of doors.

Old Bay Seasoning can be used, but I like to mix my own ingredients. I put a little beer in with the boil to give it a more pungent flavor. But the most important thing is the crab. You get only about 1 ounce of meat for every crab, so you wind up doing a lot of work and creating a big appetite. Pass around a few crab mallets and fish forks for reaching into the claws for that last piece of meat. Serve with French rolls and lots of ice-cold beer. Although this is called a crab boil, the recipe works just as well with crayfish or shrimp.

Two 12-ounce bottles beer or strong ale

8 cups cold water

I cup commercial crab-boil seasoning (or use the following seasoning)

Seasoning

¼ cup paprika

I tablespoon dry mustard

I tablespoon dried thyme

I tablespoon dried basil

I tablespoon dried oregano

1 tablespoon dried parsley

2 tablespoons cayenne

1 tablespoon salt, or to taste

1 teaspoon black pepper

2 onions, chopped

1 cup chopped scallion

1 cup chopped celery

3 whole heads garlic, crushed

3 lemons, halved

¼ cup vegetable oil

24 blue-claw crabs

12 small potatoes

3 ears fresh corn, cut into thirds

Melted butter and lemon wedges

Place a 10- or 12-quart stockpot on the grill and add the beer, water, seasonings, onion, scallion, celery, garlic, lemon halves, and vegetable oil. Bring the mixture to a boil and boil for 20 minutes. The crabs, potatoes, and corn will have to be cooked in several batches; add as many of each as will fit comfortably in the pot. The potatoes and corn will each take about 10 minutes, the crabs from 6 to 8 minutes, depending on their size. Arrange the crabs, potatoes, and corn on platters and pass lemon wedges and bowls of melted butter.

Salads

Most people don't think of salads when they picture preparing a meal on the grill, but salads are a good way to use up leftover meats, seafood, and vegetables. Just slice or chop your grilled leftovers and add them to the dish. But even when a salad is not prepared with grilled foods, it is still a great accompaniment. The recipes that follow are easy to do ahead and are ready when it comes time to serve the meal.

Stir-fry Salad
with Sesame Dressing

In Pacific Rim cuisine, the wok is the pan of choice—often because it's the only pan in the kitchen. Here we have a salad made from the vegetables you would expect to find in a stir-fried dish. For a nice touch, save the outer leaves from a Savoy or Napa cabbage, and use them as a serving dish for the salad.

> ½ head bok choy
>
> 1 cup snow peas
>
> 2 cups shredded Savoy or Napa cabbage
>
> 1 cup broccoli florets, parboiled 2 minutes
>
> ½ cup finely chopped scallion
>
> ½ red pepper, julienned
>
> 1 carrot, julienned
>
> 1 cup bean sprouts
>
> 1 recipe Sesame Dressing (page 141)
>
> ¼ cup enoki mushrooms
>
> Outer leaves of cabbage

Remove the bok choy stems and cut the stems into thin slices on an angle; shred the green leaves. Remove the strings and stems from the snow peas.

Reserve a few snow peas and some scallion for garnish.

In a large salad bowl, combine the bok choy, snow peas, cabbage, broccoli, scallion, red pepper, carrot, and bean sprouts, and toss with the Sesame Dressing. Marinate in the refrigerator for 1 hour before serving. To serve, arrange the salad on cabbage leaves and garnish with the enoki mushrooms, snow peas, and scallion.

Creole Salad

Makes 4 servings

This salad is a perfect accompaniment, both texture- and colorwise, to a grilled steak.

    8 ripe plum tomatoes, quartered

    1 sliced red onion, grilled

    1 yellow summer squash, sliced thin

    1 red bell pepper, diced

    ½ cup chopped scallion

    6 cloves Caramelized Garlic (page 111)

    1 cup Grilling Vinaigrette (page 144)

    1 head leaf lettuce, washed and drained

In a large salad bowl, combine the tomato, red onion, squash, red pepper, scallion, and Caramelized Garlic. Add the vinaigrette, toss lightly, and marinate at room temperature for 1 hour. Arrange the lettuce leaves on four salad plates and top with the salad.

Spinach Salad with Strawberries and Almonds

Makes 4 to 6 servings

I first served this salad at a summertime backyard party and it soon became everyone's favorite. The sweet honey–poppy seed dressing make a nice flavor contrast with the slightly bitter spinach and endive. Once the poppy seeds are toasted, they take on a completely different flavor.

2 bunches fresh spinach

2 heads Belgian endive

½ cup sliced mushrooms

¼ cup sliced almonds, lightly toasted

1 cup sliced strawberries

1 cup croutons

1 cup Honey-Poppy Vinaigrette (page 142)

Remove the stems from the spinach leaves and discard. Wash the spinach in cool running water until clean. Place it in a salad spinner and remove as much water as possible. (Or dry the spinach with tea towels or paper towels.) Separate the Belgian endive leaves; leave the outer leaves whole and chop the inner ones.

Arrange the spinach leaves in a shallow salad bowl. Arrange the whole outer Belgian endive leaves in a spoke fashion around the edge of the bowl. Place the chopped endive leaves in the center, and top with the mushrooms and almonds. Arrange the strawberries and croutons between the spokes of endive. Pour half the dressing over the salad and serve the remaining dressing on the side.

Green Papaya Salad

Makes 4 servings

The first time I had this salad at Keo's in Oahu, I was totally mystified by the green, vegetable-like ingredient that is central to the dish—and I was thoroughly surprised to learn that it was green papaya! The taste and texture are nothing like that of sweet ripe papaya. This is my interpretation of Keo's salad; the pungency and aroma of the chiles and lime juice make the papaya jump out at you.

1 green papaya (about ½ pound)

1 clove garlic

2 red chile peppers, seeded

1 ripe tomato, seeded and cut into strips

Juice of 2 limes

4 leaves red-leaf lettuce

1 carrot, shredded

1 cucumber, sliced

2 tablespoons chopped fresh mint leaves

Peel the papaya, cut it in half, remove the seeds, and shred the flesh. Grind or finely chop the garlic and chile peppers. Combine the papaya, garlic mixture, tomato strips, and lime juice in a small bowl and toss gently. Form each lettuce leaf into a cone shape and fill with the papaya mixture. Place on individual salad dishes and garnish with carrot, cucumber, and mint.

Grilled Peppers
and Fresh Mozzarella
with Cilantro Pesto

Makes 4 servings

The permit for new restaurants in New York must require that they have fresh mozzarella on the menu, since 99 out of 100 of them seem to. Here the milky-sweet cheese gets a Southwestern touch with the addition of Cilantro Pesto (a spin-off of basil pesto) and Tortilla Toast.

2 grilled red peppers, cut into ½-inch strips (page 18)

2 grilled yellow peppers, cut into ½-inch strips (page 18)

12 ounces fresh mozzarella, sliced

1 bunch watercress

2 tablespoons toasted pine nuts

¼ cup light olive oil

Freshly ground pepper to taste

1 recipe grilled Tortilla Toast (recipe follows)

1 recipe Cilantro Pesto (page 59)

Arrange the grilled peppers and mozzarella slices on a bed of watercress. Scatter the pine nuts on top, drizzle with olive oil, and sprinkle with pepper. Serve with Tortilla Toast and Cilantro Pesto.

Tortilla Toast

Makes 4 servings

**Grill
temperature**

medium

Four 10-inch flour tortillas

2 tablespoons vegetable oil

1 tablespoon grated Parmesan cheese

1 tablespoon chopped fresh parsley

Salt and pepper to taste

Brush the tortillas on both sides with oil and grill them quickly. Combine the cheese, parsley, salt, and pepper in a small dish. While the tortillas are still warm, cut them into triangles and dust with the cheese mixture.

Grilling

with

Chef

George

Hirsch

Cilantro Pesto

Makes about 1 cup

1 small bunch cilantro

3 cloves garlic

¼ cup walnuts

¼ cup grated Parmesan cheese

2 tablespoons sour cream

Juice of 1 lime

¼ teaspoon Tabasco sauce

½ cup olive oil

Salt and pepper to taste

Combine the cilantro, garlic, and walnuts in the bowl of a food processor, and process, using an on-off motion, until the mixture is almost smooth, pushing the mixture down with a rubber spatula, if necessary. Add the Parmesan cheese, sour cream, lime juice, and Tabasco, and process for 10 seconds. With the motor going, slowly add the olive oil. Season with salt and pepper.

Wurst Salad

This easy-to-make salad combines weisswurst, a light and delicate white veal and pork sausage seasoned with nutmeg and lemon peel, and knockwurst, a short, thick sausage made of pork, beef, garlic, and cumin. A hot salad dressing is poured over the wursts, which then marinate in the refrigerator for a few days. At that time, you may also add chunks of cooked potatoes or chopped apples. Serve with a crisp green salad, whole-grain bread, and tankards of cold beer.

½ pound knockwurst, sliced thin

½ pound weisswurst, sliced thin

2 medium red onions, sliced thin

3 or 4 bay leaves

½ cup cider vinegar

½ cup white distilled vinegar

½ cup vegetable oil

½ cup water

I cup sugar

4 whole garlic cloves

2 tablespoons mustard seed

2 whole cloves

½ teaspoon whole peppercorns

2 tablespoons chopped fresh parsley

Layer the knockwurst, weisswurst, onion slices, and bay leaves in a large bowl.

Place the remaining ingredients in a medium-size nonreactive saucepan and bring to a boil. Boil the mixture for 3 to 4 minutes; cool slightly. Pour over the wursts and refrigerate for 2 days. Drain and discard the vinegar mixture.

String Bean and
Grilled Scallop Salad

Makes 4 entree or 8 appetizer servings

The briny flavor of sea scallops and their large size make them the best choice for the grill—the sweet bay variety tend to fall into the fire. Thread the scallops onto skewers or use a porcelain grill rack. Mint and fennel seeds add interesting flavors to this salad.

I pound sea scallops

I tablespoon olive oil

½ pound string beans

½ cup vegetable oil

¼ cup balsamic vinegar

6 cloves Caramelized Garlic (page 111)

Salt and pepper to taste

½ teaspoon fennel seeds

2 tablespoons chopped fresh mint

I cup sliced mushrooms

¼ cup finely chopped red bell pepper

Lightly brush the scallops with olive oil. Remove the stems from the beans and cut the beans in half.

Parboil the string beans in lightly salted water for 8 minutes. Remove at once, drain, and immerse the beans in ice water. When cool, remove and drain well. Pat the beans dry.

Sear the scallops over high heat, scoring them with grill marks. Immediately move the scallops to a cooler edge of the grill, taking care not to overcook them. (They should cook for a maximum of 4 to 5 minutes.)

In a bowl, whisk the oil, vinegar, garlic, salt, and pepper. Stir in the fennel seed and mint.

Combine the scallops, green beans, mushrooms, and red pepper in a serving bowl. Pour the dressing over and toss lightly. Chill for 1 hour.

Grilled Chicken
Caesar Salad Santa Cruz

When I opened my restaurant, the American Bistro, four years ago, I didn't want to offer a standard Caesar salad like so many other restaurants. But we got the inevitable requests for Caesar salad and decided to come up with a new version. The Santa Cruz area in California has had a great influx of Mexicans, and the Caesar salad was originally "invented" by Caesar Cardini in Tijuana, Mexico, so we honor both here by adding grilled peppers to the salad and cumin and cilantro to the dressing. With the addition of the chicken, the salad can be served as an entree.

Four 6-ounce chicken cutlets, trimmed and lightly pounded

1 cup Southwest Marinade (page 147)

1 head red-leaf lettuce, washed

2 grilled red peppers, cut into strips (page 18)

½ cup grated Parmesan cheese

½ cup sourdough croutons

1 cup Santa Cruz Caesar Dressing (page 140)

Marinate the chicken cuttlets in the marinade for 1 hour in the refrigerator. Grill them for 5 to 6 minutes on each side, or until they are no longer pink inside; let them cool slightly. Slice the breasts very thin on an angle.

Wash the lettuce, drain, and pat dry with paper towels. Arrange the lettuce on four dinner-size plates, and arrange the chicken strips on top. Top with the grilled pepper, Parmesan cheese, and croutons. Pour ¼ cup salad dressing over each serving.

Tricolor Rotini Salad with Tomato-Gorgonzola Dressing

Makes 4 servings

Gorgonzola is the Italian equivalent of French Roquefort, but the veins are more green than blue. Gorgonzola's slightly sharp flavor blends particularly well with pasta and tomatoes.

> ½ **pound tricolor rotini**
>
> **2 tablespoons olive oil**
>
> ½ **cup black olives, sliced**
>
> **I cup cherry tomatoes, cut in half**
>
> **8 fresh basil leaves, chopped**
>
> **I cup Tomato-Gorgonzola Dressing (page 146)**
>
> **I head radicchio**

Cook the rotini according to the package directions. Drain well, combine with the oil, and chill. Combine the rotini, olives, tomatoes, basil, and dressing. Toss well and serve on radicchio leaves.

Smoked Shrimp
and Orange Salad

Makes 4 servings

When you put up the smoker, it's just as easy to smoke several types of fish at a time as it is to do only one. You might, for example, smoke some tuna steaks, a few scallops, and some shrimp. (But don't smoke fish and poultry at the same time unless you like your chicken with a faint fishy flavor.) Here's a western-style salad that's a cinch to put together once the shrimp have been smoked.

2 ripe avocados

2 naval oranges

I head red-leaf lettuce

I cucumber

I pound Smoked Shrimp (page 243)

I recipe Dijon-Horseradish Dressing (page 145)

Peel the avocados, slice them in half, remove the pits, and cut the avocados into slices. Peel the oranges and cut them horizontally into ¼-inch slices. Separate the lettuce leaves; wash and pat dry. Peel the cucumber, remove the seeds, and slice thin.

Arrange the lettuce leaves on four dinner-size plates, and arrange the avocado slices, orange slices, smoked shrimp, and cucumber slices on top. Drizzle with the dressing.

Pesto Pasta Salad

Makes 4 side-dish servings or 2 luncheon entree servings

Italians may not indulge in cold pasta, but Americans love it, especially when the pasta is tossed with good fresh tomatoes and peppery arugula. This is the kind of dish you want to eat when the weather is warm and you do your cooking in the cool morning hours. You simply open the refrigerator door at noon and your lunch is waiting. Although this recipe calls for penne, a short tubular pasta with slant-cut ends, any cut macaroni, such as ziti or rigatoni, can be used.

½ pound penne

2 tablespoons olive oil

1 cup Santa Cruz Caesar Dressing (page 140)

3 tablespoons Pesto (page 86)

3 plum tomatoes, seeded and diced

Freshly ground pepper to taste

1 bunch arugula, washed

Grated Parmesan cheese to taste (optional)

1 recipe Tuscan Toast (recipe follows)

Cook the penne according to the package instructions. Drain well, toss with the olive oil, and chill.

Combine the chilled penne, Caesar dressing, pesto, and tomato in a medium bowl, and toss gently. Season with pepper, top with arugula, and sprinkle with cheese, if desired. Serve with Tuscan Toast.

Tuscan Toast

Makes 4 servings

Grill temperature

medium

½ **cup olive oil**

2 **cloves chopped garlic**

¼ **teaspoon dried basil**

¼ **teaspoon dried thyme**

¼ **teaspoon dried oregano**

¼ **teaspoon dried parsley**

¼ **teaspoon paprika**

¼ **teaspoon ground black pepper**

I **day-old loaf Italian bread**

Combine the olive oil, garlic, basil, thyme, oregano, parsley, paprika, and black pepper in a small bowl and mix well.

Cut the Italian bread into ¾-inch slices and brush on both sides with the seasoned olive oil. Grill the bread on both sides until it has grill marks.

Warm Grapefruit Salad
with Yogurt Dressing

Makes 4 servings

Brunch dishes such as quiche or French toast often call for something light on the side. And sometimes you just want something crunchy to go along with egg dishes, which don't have much crispness. The broccoli, carrots, and nuts add the crunch; red pepper and red kidney beans add the color.

> I cup grapefruit juice
>
> 2 cups broccoli florets, parboiled 2 minutes
>
> 2 cups grapefruit sections
>
> I cup diced red bell pepper
>
> I cup thinly sliced carrot rounds
>
> One 10-ounce can kidney beans, rinsed and drained
>
> I cup raisins
>
> ½ cup toasted pecans
>
> I recipe Yogurt Dressing (page 143)

Warm the grapefruit juice in a medium saucepan. Add the broccoli, grapefruit sections, red pepper, carrots, kidney beans, raisins, and pecans, and toss gently to warm. Place the salad in a serving bowl. Pour the dressing over, toss gently, and serve.

Sweet Potato Salad
with Caper Dressing

Makes 6 to 8 servings

Potato salad usually means white potatoes, but here's one that uses sweet potatoes and has a caper dressing. The saltiness of the capers, the sweetness of the fruit juice and caramelized onions, the tartness of the vinegar, and the zip from the Tabasco combine to make a feast for the taste buds.

3 pounds sweet potatoes

2 onions, sliced

½ cup pineapple or apple juice

⅓ cup mayonnaise

⅓ cup sour cream

⅓ cup plain yogurt

⅓ cup white distilled vinegar

2 tablespoons brown sugar

I tablespoon capers, rinsed

¼ teaspoon Tabasco sauce

Pinch ground nutmeg

Salt and pepper to taste

Wash the sweet potatoes, place them in a large pot, and fill with enough cold water to cover the potatoes by 1 inch. Bring to a boil on the stovetop, lower the heat, and simmer until a knife can easily penetrate the potatoes. Or wrap sweet potatoes in foil and cook on grill. Drain the water, cool the potatoes, and chill them for 2 hours or overnight. Peel the potatoes and cut them into small pieces.

Cook the onion slices slowly on the grill (or sauté them) until they become brown and sweet; cut them into small pieces. Place the potatoes and onions in a bowl.

In a small bowl, combine the remaining ingredients and mix well. Pour the dressing over the vegetables and toss lightly.

Pepper Cabbage

This is a spin-off of coleslaw using a nonemulsified, vinegar-based dressing, which is perfect for those warm days when you worry about mayonnaise-based dressings.

I head green cabbage, chopped fine

I shredded carrot

I red bell pepper, chopped

I tablespoon finely chopped fresh parsley

I scallion, chopped

I cup sugar

¼ cup white distilled vinegar

¼ cup cider vinegar

Salt and pepper to taste

In a large bowl, combine the cabbage, carrot, red pepper, parsley, and scallion.

In a small bowl, whisk the sugar with both vinegars, salt, and pepper until well blended. Pour over the vegetables and toss lightly. Marinate for 1 hour before serving.

Pasta

Pasta is more popular than ever. In many of my grilling shows shown on PBS, we demonstrate different kinds of sauces made with grilled items that can be tossed with pasta. If the camera crew that films the show is any indication of the appeal of the pasta dishes, we never seemed to have enough on hand, so don't be afraid to make a little extra.

You can cook the pasta on the side burner of your grill (if it has one) or indoors on a conventional stovetop. One of the nice things about pasta is that you don't have to worry about keeping it piping hot. Once the pasta is drained, tossed with a little olive oil to keep the strands separate, and placed in a warm covered bowl, it should stay hot enough for the grilling table.

Spaghetti with Pesto
and Fresh Plum Tomatoes

Makes 4 servings

The flavor of plum tomatoes picked right off the vine seems to be made for pesto. Grilling the tomatoes first intensifies their flavor. This dish is simple to make and is as delicious at room temperature as it is warm.

3 plum tomatoes

1 pound spaghetti

2 tablespoons olive oil

¼ cup Pesto (page 86)

3 tablespoons grated Parmesan cheese

Freshly ground black pepper to taste

8 basil leaves for garnish

Cut the tomatoes in half and grill them for 3 to 4 minutes on each side. Remove the tomatoes from the grill and chop coarsely.

Bring 4 quarts of water to a boil and cook the spaghetti al dente, according to the package directions. Drain well.

Place the spaghetti in a large bowl and toss with the olive oil. Add the tomatoes and the pesto and toss again. Divide the spaghetti among four serving dishes and sprinkle with Parmesan cheese and black pepper. Garnish with basil leaves.

Gnocchi with Ricotta and Smoked Mozzarella

Makes 4 servings

Gnocchi, potato dumplings, are available at local pasta stores or in supermarket freezers. When the ricotta and smoked mozzarella are tossed with the hot gnocchi, they melt and make the sauce—nothing could be simpler.

I pound gnocchi

¼ cup olive oil

6 to 8 basil leaves, chopped

Freshly ground black pepper to taste

2 cups ricotta

4 ounces smoked mozzarella, diced

I cup seeded and chopped plum tomatoes

5 to 6 cloves Caramelized Garlic (page I I I)

Pinch ground nutmeg

Bring 6 quarts of water to a boil on grill or stovetop and add the gnocchi. When the water returns to a simmer, cook the gnocchi until they all float, about 4 to 5 minutes. Drain well and toss with the olive oil, basil, and black pepper.

In a medium bowl, combine the ricotta, mozzarella, tomato, garlic, and nutmeg. Add the hot drained gnocchi and toss gently.

Linguine with Clams, Mussels, and Squid

Makes 4 servings

Grill temperature

medium-high

Cooking seafood outdoors during the warm-weather months seems to be a natural. You can add extra flavor to this dish by leaving the squid whole and grilling them on the fire very quickly. The sauce is a combination of the natural juices from the seafood, white wine, and butter. What could be better?

I pound linguine

2 cups dry white wine

¼ pound (1 stick) butter

6 cloves Caramelized Garlic (page 111), chopped

¼ cup chopped Italian parsley

I teaspoon red pepper flakes

2 pounds mussels, cleaned and debearded

I dozen littleneck clams, scrubbed

I pound squid, cut into rings

Bring 4 quarts of water to a boil and cook the linguine al dente according to the package directions. Drain well and keep warm.

Place the wine, butter, garlic, parsley, and red pepper flakes in a large stockpot and place it on the grill. When the butter melts, add the mussels and clams and cover tightly. Cook the seafood for 6 to 8 minutes, shaking the pot frequently, or until the shells open. Remove the mussels and clams, discarding any that remain closed. Add the squid to the cooking liquid and simmer for 2 minutes. Remove the squid and add to the clams and mussels. Boil the liquid for 1 minute and toss with the cooked linguine. Divide the pasta among four serving dishes and top with the seafood

Penne with Roasted Eggplant, Red Peppers, Lemon, and Basil

Makes 4 servings

The caramelized flavor of the grilled vegetables makes this sauce exceptionally tasty. The eggplant gives a full rounded taste to this dish and makes it appealing to vegetarians. It is equally good hot or at room temperature.

I eggplant, sliced lengthwise into ¼-inch slices

2 red bell peppers, cut into 1-inch strips

I lemon, cut into ¼-inch slices

¼ cup olive oil

I pound penne

2 tablespoons butter

2 tablespoons olive oil

4 to 5 cloves Caramelized Garlic (page 111)

Salt and freshly ground black pepper to taste

Grated Parmesan cheese to taste

2 basil leaves, coarsely chopped

Brush the eggplant, pepper, and lemon slices with ¼ cup olive oil. Place the vegetables on the grill and cook them until they're light brown on both sides. Cut into 1-inch pieces. Combine all the vegetables in a bowl and keep warm.

Bring 6 quarts of water to a boil on grill or stovetop and cook the penne al dente, according to the package directions. Drain well and place in a serving bowl. Toss the pasta with the butter, 2 tablespoons olive oil, and garlic, and season with salt and pepper. Add the grilled vegetables and toss gently. Top with Parmesan cheese and basil leaves.

Grilled Chicken
with Orecchiette

Makes 4 servings

Orecchiette, which means "little ears," is fast becoming a popular pasta. If you can't find it at the supermarket, use any small pasta, such as shells or penne. The addition of 2 cups of cream makes this a decadent, and delicious, recipe.

½ **tablespoon dried basil**

3 **cloves garlic**

¼ **teaspoon Tabasco sauce**

¼ **teaspoon Worcestershire sauce**

Four 6-ounce boneless and skinless chicken breasts

1 **pound orecchiette**

2 **cups chicken stock**

2 **cups heavy cream**

4 **ounces Gorgonzola cheese, crumbled**

3 **tablespoons grated Parmesan cheese**

¼ **cup pecans, smoked or toasted**

8 **whole basil leaves**

Combine the dried basil, garlic, Tabasco, and Worcestershire sauce in a small bowl, and marinate the chicken in this mixture for 2 hours in the refrigerator. Grill the chicken for 5 to 6 minutes on each side, and cut it into ½-inch strips.

Bring 6 quarts of water to a boil on grill or stovetop. Cook the orecchiette according to the package directions and drain well.

Heat the chicken stock in a pot large enough to hold the pasta. Add the cream and half of the Gorgonzola. Bring the mixture to a boil on grill or stovetop. Add the pasta, stir well, and heat until warm. Stir in the remaining Gorgonzola, Parmesan cheese, and pecans. Divide the pasta among four dishes, top with the grilled chicken strips, and garnish with basil leaves.

Fettuccine with Grilled Shrimp and Walnut Pesto

Makes 4 servings

This is a great way to use leftover grilled shrimp (and using leftovers makes this recipe go a lot faster), but even if you have to start from scratch by marinating the shrimp, I think you'll find it's well worth the effort.

½ pound large shrimp (16 to 20 per pound)

1 recipe Cane-Charred Marinade (page 194)

1 pound fettuccine

2 tablespoons olive oil

¼ cup Walnut Pesto (recipe follows)

2 cups fish (page 33) or chicken (page 32) stock

¼ cup heavy cream

Salt and pepper to taste

3 tablespoons grated Parmesan cheese (optional)

2 tablespoons chopped scallion

Presoak 4 wooden skewers in water for 1 hour. Peel the shrimp, leaving the tails intact; devein the shrimp and thread them on the skewers. Marinate the shrimp in the Cane-Charred Marinade for 1 hour in the refrigerator. Grill them, turning them once, for 5 to 6 minutes, or until they turn opaque and the shells brown slightly.

Bring 4 quarts of water to a boil and cook the fettuccine al dente, according to the package directions. Drain well and toss with the olive oil.

Place the Walnut Pesto in a saucepan on the grill or stovetop. Add the stock and bring to a boil; add the cream and the grilled shrimp. Season with salt and pepper. Toss half of the sauce with the fettuccine. Divide the pasta among four dishes and top with the remaining sauce. Sprinkle with Parmesan cheese and scallion.

Walnut Pesto

Makes about 1 1/2 cups

If you toast the walnuts first, the pesto will have a more intense flavor. Don't overprocess the pesto or the mixture will be pasty.

1 cup shelled walnuts

5 cloves garlic

1/4 cup packed fresh basil leaves

1/4 cup packed fresh Italian parsley

1/3 cup olive oil

3 tablespoons grated Parmesan cheese

Combine the walnuts and garlic in the food processor and coarsely grind them using an on-off motion. Add the basil and parsley and process until almost smooth, scraping down the sides when necessary. With the motor going, slowly add the oil and the cheese. Process for 30 seconds; do not overmix.

Cavatelli with
White Beans and Escarole

Makes 4 servings

Grill
temperature

high for
grilling the
onion and
escarole,
then
medium-high

Cavatelli is a rippled pasta shell that is sometimes called dry gnocchi. This shape goes especially well with broths and sauces with lots of liquid. Make sure you wash the escarole well and remove all the sand. Grilling the escarole first subtly changes its flavor.

1 onion, sliced

2 tablespoons olive oil

½ head escarole, washed

1 pound cavatelli

¼ cup olive oil

10 to 12 cloves Caramelized Garlic (page 111)

½ lemon, sliced thin

½ tablespoon red pepper flakes (optional)

¼ teaspoon Tabasco sauce

¼ teaspoon dried basil

2 cups chicken or vegetable stock

Salt and pepper to taste

¼ cup grated Parmesan cheese

Brush the onion slices with 1 tablespoon of the olive oil and grill for 5 minutes on each side; chop coarsely. Rinse the escarole well, sprinkle with 1 tablespoon of olive oil, and place on the very hot grill for 15 seconds on each side; chop coarsely.

Bring 4 quarts of water to a boil and cook the cavatelli al dente, according to the package directions. Drain well and keep warm.

Heat the ¼ cup olive oil in a large black cast-iron skillet or stockpot on the grill or stovetop. Add the garlic and lemon, and sauté for 2 minutes. Quickly stir in the pepper flakes, Tabasco, basil, grilled onion, and escarole; cover and cook for 1 minute. Uncover and add the cavatelli, chicken stock, salt, and pepper. Bring to a simmer and serve in soup bowls. Sprinkle with Parmesan cheese.

Pesto

I always wind up using a lot of pesto during the summer, especially when there's a great crop of basil. I like to add a touch of Italian parsley to give the pesto a greener color, but unless the parsley is very fresh, don't add too much or your pesto will end up tasting like grass clippings. Cover the pesto with ½ inch of olive oil, and store it in the refrigerator for a few weeks, or freeze it.

Pesto making is a great job for the food processor, and there are all sorts of pesto spin-offs if you use your imagination.

6 cloves garlic

3 tablespoons pine nuts or walnuts

¾ cup packed fresh basil leaves, washed and dried

¼ cup fresh Italian parsley (optional)

½ cup grated Parmesan cheese

½ cup olive oil

Place the garlic and nuts in the bowl of a food processor and process for 10 seconds. Add the basil and parsley and process for 20 seconds. Add the cheese and process for 10 seconds. With the motor going, slowly add the olive oil.

Linguine with Sea Scallops and Grilled Pepper Pesto

Makes 4 servings

Using grilled red bell peppers in the pesto makes this dish a bright red and sets off the green jalapeño peppers. The dish is a little sweet, a little hot, and a little smoky. The sea scallops can be slipped off the skewers or left on the skewers and laid over the pasta.

1 ½ **pounds sea scallops**

1 **recipe Cane-Charred Marinade (page 194)**

1 **pound linguine**

¼ **cup Grilled Pepper Pesto (recipe follows)**

2 **tablespoons olive oil**

2 **jalapeño peppers, seeded and sliced thin**

1 **tablespoon chopped cilantro**

3 **tablespoons grated Parmesan cheese (optional)**

Marinate the sea scallops in the Cane-Charred Marinade for 1 hour in the refrigerator. Remove the scallops from the marinade, thread them onto skewers, and grill them until they are opaque, about 4 to 5 minutes.

Bring 4 quarts of water to a boil and cook the linguine al dente, according to the package directions. Drain well and return to the pot; add the pesto, olive oil, and scallops, and toss gently. Arrange on four plates and top with jalapeño, cilantro, and Parmesan cheese.

Grilled Pepper Pesto

Makes about I cup

Use either all red, green, or yellow bell peppers. This pesto make a colorful addition to Southwestern-style pastas and meats. If you would like a sharper taste, use cilantro instead of parsley.

6 cloves garlic

2 tablespoons walnuts

I cup grilled peppers, peeled (page 18)

¼ cup fresh Italian parsley or cilantro

¼ cup grated Parmesan cheese

¼ cup olive oil

Place the garlic and walnuts in the bowl of a food processor and process for 10 seconds. Add the peppers and parsley and process for 20 seconds. Add the cheese and process for 10 seconds. With the motor going, slowly add the olive oil.

Spaghetti with
Caramelized Garlic and Oil

Makes 3 to 4 entree servings or 6 to 8 appetizer servings

Caramelized garlic is totally different in flavor from raw garlic. Roasting brings out a nutty, almost sweet, flavor with no aftertaste. Here is a dish that goes as well with steak as it does with grilled vegetables.

I pound spaghetti

8 tablespoons olive oil

3 whole heads Caramelized Garlic (page 111)

¼ cup (½ stick) butter (optional)

¼ cup bread crumbs

4 to 5 fresh basil leaves, chopped

¼ cup grated Parmesan cheese

Salt and pepper to taste

Bring 4 quarts of water to a boil and cook the spaghetti al dente, according to the package directions. Drain well, toss with 2 tablespoons of olive oil, and keep warm.

Squeeze the garlic out from the individual cloves and place in a 1-quart saucepan with the remaining 6 tablespoons olive oil and the butter, stirring until well combined. Warm this mixture on the grill and stir in the bread crumbs, basil, Parmesan cheese, salt, and pepper.

Immediately toss with the spaghetti and serve at once. Sprinkle with additional cheese, if desired.

Fettuccine with Leeks, Mushrooms, and Crayfish

Makes 4 servings

Grill
temperature

medium,
then low

Although this dish may not sound very Cajun, it does use Cajun-style flavorings and seasonings. If you can't find crayfish, use shrimp or mussels. The mushrooms give this dish a nice earthy taste, and the pecans provide a great contrast in texture. This is a very rich dish and a delight to the eye, but to lower the calories, you can leave out the cream.

I pound fettuccine

4 tablespoons olive oil

I leek, white part only, chopped

6 cloves Caramelized Garlic (page 111)

I cup sliced mushrooms (button, cremini, or shiitake)

I cup peeled and seeded plum tomatoes

4 cups fish (page 33) or chicken (page 32) stock

I pound cooked crayfish or shrimp

2 cups heavy cream or I additional cup stock

I tablespoon chopped fresh thyme

¼ teaspoon Tabasco sauce

¼ cup smoked or toasted pecans, chopped

Bring 4 quarts of water to a boil and cook the fettuccine al dente, according to the package directions. Drain well and toss with 2 tablespoons of olive oil.

Heat a saucepan on the grill over medium heat and add the remaining 2 tablespoons of olive oil. Stir in the leek and garlic, and cook until the leek is transparent, 2 to 3 minutes. Stir in the mushrooms, tomato, and stock, and cook for 4 to 5 minutes. Stir in the crayfish, cream or stock, thyme, and Tabasco. Bring to a boil, season with salt and pepper, lower the heat, and simmer for 2 to 3 minutes. Toss with the fettuccine and sprinkle with pecans.

Grilled Polenta

Makes 6 to 8 servings

Trying to explain grilled polenta to a group of people in the South, I called it "hard grits," and they got the message. When polenta is hot, it should have a custardlike consistency, but once it has been chilled, cut into wedges, brushed with olive oil, and grilled, it gets a nice crust on the outside while remaining creamy inside.

Polenta is bland by nature, but it's given its due by what it's served with. Try it with grilled Portobello mushrooms, stews, chili, lamb, pasta sauces, or any dish that contains a very flavorful sauce. My Italian grandfather, whom I like to call the "King of Polenta," is ninety-two, and polenta is the one dish my grandmother allowed him to make.

(continued)

Grill temperature

medium

91

Pasta

2 cups milk

2 cups water

I cup finely ground yellow cornmeal

2 tablespoons chopped fresh basil

2 tablespoons grated Parmesan cheese

I teaspoon Tabasco sauce

I teaspoon salt

2 tablespoons olive oil

In a medium-size heavy saucepan, bring the milk and water to a boil on the grill or stovetop. Slowly add the cornmeal, stirring constantly. Cook over low heat for 30 to 35 minutes, stirring constantly. Add the basil, Parmesan cheese, Tabasco, and salt, and mix well. Pour the mixture into a lightly greased 10-inch round cake pan and allow to cool.

To serve, slice the polenta into wedges, brush with olive oil, and grill on both sides until golden brown.

Penne with Sausage
and Grilled Peppers

Makes 4 servings

**Grill
temperature**

medium

Sausage with grilled peppers is one of those standard backyard grilling dishes, but when you toss it with al dente penne, it winds up being a delightful summer meal and the kind that makes everyone ask for seconds.

Use all hot sausage, all sweet sausage, or half of each. To keep the onion slices intact while grilling, insert two toothpicks, one in each side of the slices.

> **I pound Italian-style sausage**
>
> **6 to 8 long thin Italian frying peppers**
>
> **I small red onion, sliced ¼ inch thick**
>
> **6 cloves Caramelized Garlic (page I I I)**
>
> **I pound penne**
>
> **¼ cup olive oil**
>
> **2 tablespoons chopped fresh basil**
>
> **Grated Parmesan cheese to taste**

Grill the sausages until almost cooked, about 30 minutes. Remove them and set them aside to cool. Split the peppers in half lengthwise and remove the seeds. Place the peppers on the grill with the onion slices, and grill until lightly charred, about 15 minutes. When the sausages are cool, slice them into 1-inch pieces and place them in a saucepan on the grill or stovetop with the peppers, onion, and Caramelized Garlic, and cook until the sausages are no longer pink inside.

Bring 6 quarts of water to a boil and cook the penne according to package directions. Drain and combine with the olive oil in a large pasta bowl. Spoon the sausage mixture on top and toss lightly. Sprinkle with basil and Parmesan cheese.

Pizza

Cooking pizza on a grill is really simple once you get the knack—it just takes some experimenting. If you don't have the time to make your own pizza dough, it's readily available in the frozen-foods section of your local grocery or perhaps from your local pizzeria or bakery.

However, there's nothing like making pizza dough from scratch. It's a simple combination of flour, sugar, yeast, oil, and water. The technique does require a bit of trial and error, but it's well worth it. Make the dough ahead of time and refrigerate it. This will enable the dough to develop flavor and to relax properly so that when you roll it out, it won't shrink up on you.

Grilled pizzas cook very fast, so have your toppings precooked and ready before you place the dough on the grill. Gas grills with carbon steel or porcelain grids work best because there is less chance of the dough sticking. You can also use round metal pizza screens.

I've cooked thousands of different pizzas, both at commercial events and at backyard affairs, and the lines of people ready to eat form faster than you can feed them.

Pizza Dough

Enough dough for 2 to 3 pizzas

The pizza disks can be made in advance. Make the dough (I've given three methods of mixing it), grill the pizzas on one side, wrap well, and freeze. To defrost, unwrap the pizza disks and leave them at room temperature for 15 to 20 minutes.

I teaspoon active dry yeast

¼ cup warm water (between 105° and 115°F.)

I teaspoon sugar

3 ½ cups bread flour or all-purpose flour

¼ teaspoon salt

¾ cup warm water

I tablespoon olive oil

In a small bowl, combine the yeast and water; add the sugar and stir well. Set aside for 10 minutes, or until small bubbles appear on the surface.

Using an electric mixer with a dough hook

In the large bowl of a heavy-duty electric mixer with a dough hook, combine 3 cups of the flour and the salt. Pour in the yeast mixture and the warm water and stir until blended. Set the dough hook in place and, with the mixer at medium speed, knead the dough for 8 minutes, adding the additional ½ cup flour if the dough is sticky.

Using a food processor

Place 3¼ cups of the flour and salt in the bowl of a food processor, and with the motor going, slowly pour in the yeast mixture and the water. Process for 40 seconds, or until the mixture is smooth. If the dough is too wet, add 1 tablespoon of flour at a time and process until just combined.

By hand

Place 3 cups of the flour in a mixing bowl. Make a well in the center and pour in the yeast mixture and the water. Stir with a wooden spoon until the dough comes together. Turn the dough out onto a lightly floured surface and knead for 10 minutes, using the additional ½ cup flour if the dough is sticky.

Regardless of which method is used, the dough is sufficiently kneaded when you can stick two fingers into it and it springs back without leaving an indentation.

Cut the dough into four pieces and roll each piece into a ball. Let the dough rest in an oiled bowl for 45 to 60 minutes. Lightly oil the top of each ball with the 1 tablespoon olive oil, cover with plastic wrap, and place in the refrigerator for 3 hours.

To Grill the Pizza

Sprinkle a wooden pizza peel with cornmeal. Place a ball of dough in the center of the peel. Flatten ball or the dough into an 8- to 10-inch disk, using your fingertips or a rolling pin. Brush the dough with olive oil and poke a few holes in it with a fork. Hold the peel over the grill, and with a quick jerk, pull the peel away, allowing the dough to drop onto the clean, hot grill. Grill for approximately 2 minutes, or until the dough begins to bubble.

(An alternative method is to coat the bottom of a cookie pan with a little oil and flatten the dough on the pan with your fingertips or a rolling pin. With the dough as close as possible to the grill, lift the dough with your fingers and quickly transfer it to the clean, hot grill. Grill for approximately 2 minutes, or until the dough begins to bubble.) Lift a corner of the pizza with tongs, and when grill marks appear, remove it from the grill, turn it over, and arrange the toppings on the cooked side. Return the pizza to the grill for another 2 minutes with the hood down. Raise the hood and lift a corner of the pizza with tongs. If it begins to get too dark, move it to a cooler edge of the grill.

You can also place a pizza stone on the grill and bake the pizza on that, or you can cover the pizza with a ceramic dome to help the top of the crust brown and the cheese melt.

Variations

Whole-Wheat Pizza Dough

Using these ingredients, follow the directions for making pizza dough.

1 ½ teaspoons active dry yeast

¼ cup warm water (between 105° and 115°F.)

½ tablespoon honey

3 cups whole-wheat flour

½ cup bread flour

¼ teaspoon salt

¾ cup warm water

1 tablespoon olive oil

Garlic Pizza Dough

Follow the directions for making pizza dough (page 96) and mix the basil, black pepper, garlic, and oil with the 3 cups flour. This dough makes great deep-dish pizzas, focaccias or Garlic Knots.

Grill temperature

medium

½ teaspoon active dry yeast

¼ cup warm water (between 105° and 115°F.)

1 teaspoon sugar

3 ½ cups bread flour

¼ teaspoon salt

½ teaspoon dried basil

¼ teaspoon coarsely ground black pepper

4 cloves Caramelized Garlic (page 111)

2 tablespoons olive oil

To make deep-dish pizza, or focaccia, cut the dough in half and flatten each half into a 6-inch disk, approximately ½ inch thick. Lightly oil two 7-inch pie pans. Flatten both disks, place them in the pie pans, and grill for 8 to 10 minutes. Brush the tops with oil, turn the dough over in the pans, and grill for 5 to 6 minutes longer. Turn the disks over again, cover them with pizza or focaccia toppings, and grill 2 to 3 minutes longer.

Garlic Knots

Makes 20 to 24

Grill temperature

medium

I recipe Garlic Pizza Dough (page 99)

¼ cup olive oil

¼ cup grated Parmesan cheese

I teaspoon dried basil

I teaspoon dried parsley

I teaspoon sesame seeds (optional)

Red pepper flakes to taste (optional)

¼ teaspoon sea salt (optional)

Spread the dough into an 8- by 12-inch rectangle. Cut with a knife into 20 to 24 pieces. Roll each piece into a 6-inch rope and tie each rope into a loose knot. Place on an oiled tray, cover with a tea towel, and place in a warm place for 10 to 15 minutes.

When the knots have doubled in size, brush them with some of the olive oil. Place them in a metal pan or on foil, and place on the grill and cover with the hood. After 5 to 6 minutes, turn them over and bake 6 to 8 minutes longer. The bottoms should have a hollow sound when tapped with a finger.

In a large bowl, mix the remaining olive oil, Parmesan cheese, basil, parsley, sesame seeds, red pepper flakes, and sea salt. Add the garlic knots and toss gently.

Italian Pizza Sauce

Makes about 2 cups

This is a traditional recipe for pizza sauce and the universal favorite. Use fresh plum tomatoes or canned crushed plum tomatoes. (Avoid salad tomatoes, as they're too watery.)

> **2 cups crushed Italian plum tomatoes, fresh or canned**
>
> **¼ cup chopped onion**
>
> **5 cloves Caramelized Garlic (page 111)**
>
> **6 basil leaves, chopped, or 1 teaspoon dried basil**
>
> **½ teaspoon dried oregano**
>
> **Salt and pepper to taste**

Combine all of the ingredients in a 2-quart saucepan and simmer for 4 to 5 minutes, stirring occasionally.

Barbecue Pizza Sauce

Here's a tomato sauce with a sweet-and-sour twist.

> 2 cups crushed Italian plum tomatoes
>
> 3 cloves Caramelized Garlic (page 111)
>
> 2 tablespoons honey
>
> 2 tablespoons cider vinegar
>
> 1 tablespoon brown sugar
>
> ½ teaspoon dried thyme
>
> ¼ teaspoon Worcestershire sauce
>
> ¼ teaspoon Tabasco sauce
>
> Salt and pepper to taste

In a 2-quart saucepan, combine all of the ingredients. Bring to a boil, lower the heat, and simmer for 4 to 5 minutes, stirring occasionally.

102

Grilling
with
Chef
George
Hirsch

Pesto Pizza Sauce

Mascarpone is the thick, rich Italian cheese used in tiramisù. You can usually find it in a cheese shop or Italian deli, but if none is available, substitute ⅔ cup softened cream cheese and ⅓ cup sour cream.

> ½ **cup heavy cream**
>
> I **cup mascarpone**
>
> I **cup ricotta**
>
> ¼ **cup Pesto (page 86)**

In a medium bowl, combine all of the ingredients and mix well.

Bianca Pizza Sauce

Makes about 2 cups

You'll want to use this sauce on an all-white pizza or on a pizza with delicate toppings such as smoked salmon or mascarpone.

> **I cup mascarpone (or ⅔ cup softened cream cheese and ⅓ cup sour cream)**
> **I cup heavy cream**
> **I tablespoon hazelnut liqueur or sherry**
> **2 tablespoons chopped shallot or onion**

In a medium bowl, combine all of the ingredients and mix well.

Peanut Pizza Sauce

Makes about I ½ cups

Few will guess that the secret ingredient in this sauce is peanut butter.

> **I cup chunky peanut butter**
> **¼ cup pineapple juice or water**
> **I teaspoon chopped cilantro**
> **¼ cup chopped scallion**
> **¼ teaspoon Tabasco sauce**

In a medium bowl, combine all of the ingredients and mix well.

104

Grilling
with
Chef
George
Hirsch

Three-Cheese Pizza

Makes 4 servings

When the Gorgonzola melts, it becomes creamy and gives the pizza a nutty flavor that complements the toastiness of the pecans.

Because of the intense flavor of the toppings, this pizza needs no base sauce. Serve it as a luncheon entree or dinner appetizer. It goes exceptionally well with greens tossed with olive oil.

1 recipe Whole-wheat Pizza Dough (page 98)

½ cup shredded mozzarella

½ cup crumbled Gorgonzola

½ cup chèvre, sliced

2 red onions, sliced and grilled over medium heat until tender

¼ cup toasted pecans or walnuts

2 tablespoons grated Parmesan cheese

4 basil leaves, coarsely chopped

Follow the directions for making pizza on a grill (page 97). When the pizza is cooked on one side, turn it over and place the mozzarella, Gorgonzola, and chèvre on top. Cover with grilled onion slices and pecans. Grill the pizza for 2 minutes, or until the cheeses melt. Sprinkle with Parmesan and chopped basil.

Cajun Pizza

Makes 4 servings

Grilled andouille sausage and grilled pepper strips pack this pizza with lots of flavor. Andouille is a Cajun-style smoked pork sausage; if you have trouble finding it, substitute kielbasa.

> **1 recipe Garlic Pizza Dough (page 99)**
> **8 ounces andouille sausage, sliced lengthwise and grilled over high**
> **heat until hot**
> **1 cup shredded mozzarella**
> **¼ cup chopped scallion**
> **½ cup roasted peppers, cut into strips**
> **¼ teaspoon ground thyme**
> **¼ teaspoon ground coriander**
> **¼ teaspoon paprika**
> **Ground black pepper to taste**
> **Tabasco sauce to taste**

Follow the directions for making pizza on the grill (page 97). When the pizza is cooked on one side, turn it over and top it with the sausage, mozzarella, scallion, and roasted peppers. Sprinkle with thyme, coriander, paprika, black pepper, and Tabasco. Grill the pizza for 2 minutes, or until the cheese melts.

Fresh Plum Tomato
and Fresh Mozzarella Pizza

Makes 4 servings

This is the classic Italian pizza. The fresh mozzarella becomes sweet and milky on the grill.

 1 recipe Pizza Dough (page 96)

 1 cup Italian Pizza Sauce (page 101)

 3 large fresh plum tomatoes, sliced

 1 pound fresh mozzarella cheese, cut into 16 slices

 2 tablespoons grated Parmesan cheese

 4 basil leaves, chopped

Divide the dough into four equal portions.

Follow the directions for making pizza on the grill (pages 97–98). When the pizzas are cooked on one side, turn them over and spread each round with ¼ cup pizza sauce, leaving a ½-inch space around the edges. Top with layers of tomato and mozzarella. Return to the grill for about 2 minutes or until the mozzarella melts. Remove and sprinkle with Parmesan cheese and basil.

Other Pizza Combinations to Try

Cane-Charred Shrimp with Peanut Sauce

Smoked salmon, Bianca Sauce, and scallions

Grilled sliced chicken breast, Pesto Sauce, and walnuts

Smoked ham and Barbecue Pizza Sauce

Trio of mushrooms (shiitake, Portobello, cremini) and Bianca Sauce

Roasted jalapeño peppers, Bianca Sauce, and sun-dried tomatoes

Grilled eggplant and Italian Pizza Sauce

Focaccia Toppings

Olive oil, shallots, and scallions

Dried rosemary and thyme

Green and black olives

Sun-dried tomatoes and fresh basil leaves

Caramelized Garlic and crushed black peppercorns

Vegetables

Whenever I travel to different cities and states, I make it a point to visit the local supermarkets, and I'm always amazed at the variety of produce available. It used to be that only restaurant chefs had access to produce not available in supermarkets, but this is no longer true. No matter where I go, most well-stocked supermarkets now offer a great array of fresh herbs, fresh vegetables, and wild mushrooms. All you have to do is walk down a produce department aisle to decide what to put on the grill.

How to Cook Dried Beans and Legumes

Spread the beans on a flat surface and look them over. Remove any broken ones or bits of stone and twigs.

There are two ways of cooking dried legumes. The first is to place them in a large pot, cover them with a few inches of water, bring the water to a boil, and boil the legumes for 2 minutes. Remove the pot from the stove and let it sit for 1 hour. Drain off the water, cover the legumes with fresh water, and bring the water to a boil. Lower the heat and simmer the legumes for about 1 hour, or until tender.

The second way is to cover the legumes with water and allow them to soak for 8 hours, or overnight. Drain off the water, cover with fresh water, and cook for 1 hour, or until tender.

The amount of time it takes different legumes to cook varies—chickpeas take longer than kidney beans, for example. And the age of the bean is a consideration—the older the bean, the longer it takes to cook.

Caramelized Garlic

6 heads garlic

Using caramelized garlic instead of butter on bread saves lots of calories—it also tastes delicious! Caramelized garlic can be substituted for fresh garlic in most recipes. Add a few heads of garlic whenever there's room for them on the grill. Cover the cooked heads with a little olive oil, cover well, and refrigerate for later use.

6 heads garlic

¼ cup olive oil

One 12-inch square aluminum foil

Slice off ¼ inch from the bottom of each head of garlic. (This makes it easier to remove the garlic after it has been caramelized.)

Rub the garlic with olive oil and place on the grill, cut side down. Cook very slowly, allowing the natural sugars to caramelize. (The total cooking time should be between 45 and 60 minutes.) Halfway through, cover the garlic with the foil.

Montauk Indian
Corn on the Cob

Makes 4 servings

Grill
temperature

medium

The fresher the corn, the better the flavor. Once corn is picked, the sugar starts turning to starch, and the corn begins to lose its sweetness. For a very special flavor, cover the kernels with a few strips of bacon before repositioning the husks.

4 ears fresh corn

2 tablespoons vegetable oil

4 tablespoons (½ stick) butter, melted

Sea salt and freshly ground black pepper to taste

Four 12-inch squares aluminum foil

Pull the corn husks back, but do not remove them. Remove and discard the corn silk. Combine the oil and butter and brush the corn with this mixture. Season with salt and pepper. Reposition the corn husks over the kernels and wrap each ear individually in aluminum foil. Grill for 20 minutes, turning frequently.

112

Grilling
with
Chef
George
Hirsch

Grilled Asparagus

Makes 4 servings

Asparagus certainly are the harbingers of spring, and maybe that's why they go so well with lamb for Easter dinner. At other times of the year, serve asparagus with grilled chicken, salmon, or shrimp, or chill them and serve as part of a salad.

Grill temperature

medium

> **I pound asparagus**
>
> **½ cup olive oil**
>
> **Juice and zest of I lemon**
>
> **6 cloves Caramelized Garlic (page I I I)**
>
> **¼ teaspoon dried rosemary or leaves of I sprig fresh rosemary, chopped**

Cut the stem ends off the asparagus and discard; peel the asparagus up to the beginning of the tip ends with a vegetable peeler. Parboil the asparagus until bright green, about 2 minutes. (Or place in a covered dish and microwave on high for 1½ minutes.)

Combine the olive oil, lemon juice, garlic, and rosemary in a shallow rectangular dish. Marinate the asparagus in this mixture for 1 hour. Remove the asparagus from the marinade and grill for 10 minutes, basting with the marinade.

Cajun Onions

Makes 6 servings

Cajun food is flavorful, but it should not be so hot that it overpowers your taste buds or burns your mouth. For those who want their food extra hot, leave a bottle of hot sauce on the table. Serve these onions with steaks and pork chops as an alternative to fried onions. For a low-cholesterol version, substitute 2 tablespoons of olive oil for the butter. There are a few good Cajun seasoning blends on the market that can be substituted for the spices (use 2¼ teaspoons).

Grill temperature

high, then low

3 large onions, sliced ¼ inch thick

One 12- by 24-inch piece heavy-duty aluminum foil

½ cup (1 stick) butter, softened

1 teaspoon paprika

¼ teaspoon garlic powder

¼ teaspoon dried oregano

¼ teaspoon dried thyme

¼ teaspoon black pepper

¼ teaspoon ground nutmeg

Pinch white pepper

½ teaspoon Tabasco sauce

¼ teaspoon Worcestershire sauce

114

Grilling

with

Chef

George

Hirsch

Place the onion slices in the center of the foil. Combine the remaining ingredients and stir until well combined. Dot the onions with the seasoned butter and wrap in foil, folding the edges over twice. Place the packets on a hot grill for 3 to 5 minutes on each side; move them to low heat for 10 minutes longer.

These onions can also be cooked in a black cast-iron skillet. Melt the butter in a skillet and stir in the spices. Add the onions and cook over high heat until the onions are limp; move the pan to lower heat.

Stuffed Tomatoes with Spinach

Makes 4 servings

Stuffed tomatoes are a good way to use up the garden's bounty, but any fresh vegetable, such as zucchini or peppers, can be substituted. Grilling the tomatoes in foil nests helps them keep their shape.

**Grill
temperature**

medium

4 large tomatoes

Four 14-inch squares heavy-duty foil for making nests

Stuffing

**One 10-ounce package frozen spinach, thawed, or 1 cup cooked fresh
spinach**

1 small onion, diced fine

4 cloves Caramelized Garlic (page 111)

¼ teaspoon ground nutmeg

Salt and pepper to taste

2 tablespoons grated Parmesan cheese

2 tablespoons bread crumbs

Cut a slice from the stem end of each tomato. Remove the pulp and seeds with a teaspoon and reserve. Invert the tomatoes and drain on paper towels.

In a medium bowl, combine the reserved tomato pulp, the spinach, onion, garlic, nutmeg, salt, and pepper. Spoon the mixture back into the tomato halves and sprinkle with Parmesan cheese and bread crumbs. Fashion a nest with each square of foil and place a tomato in each one. Grill for 15 minutes.

116

Grilling
with
Chef
George
Hirsch

Grilled Corn and
Tomatoes with Beans

Makes 6 to 8 servings

This is a variation of succotash, a traditional Native American dish combining lima beans and corn. Serve it warm as a side dish or chilled as a salad. Or add 4 cups of vegetable or chicken stock and a 6-ounce can of tomato sauce to the dish and simmer for 20 minutes for an American-style minestrone.

> **I recipe Montauk Indian Corn on the Cob (page 112)**
>
> **2 large ripe tomatoes, cut into 1-inch pieces**
>
> **One 16-ounce can cannellini beans, rinsed and drained, or 8 ounces**
> **cooked dried white beans**
>
> **2 cloves Caramelized Garlic (page 111)**
>
> **¼ cup olive oil**
>
> **½ teaspoon chopped cilantro**
>
> **½ teaspoon dried basil**
>
> **Salt and pepper to taste**

Cut the kernels off the cobs and place them in a medium bowl with the remaining ingredients. Toss gently.

117

Black-eyed Peas and Greens

Makes 4 servings

This is a typical dish of the Deep South. Almost any bitter greens, such as mustard or collard greens, can be used. Black-eyed peas, sometimes called cowpeas, are traditionally served in the South on New Year's Eve to ensure prosperity during the coming year.

2 cups cooked black-eyed peas

I medium onion, diced

4 cloves Caramelized Garlic (page III)

¼ cup finely diced bacon

I cup diced smoked sausage (such as andouille or kielbasa)

½ cup diced celery

½ cup chopped scallion

2 cups chicken stock

½ teaspoon Tabasco sauce

½ teaspoon Worcestershire sauce

Salt and pepper to taste

Leaves from I bunch Swiss chard, washed and chopped

118

Grilling
with
Chef
George
Hirsch

Place all of the ingredients except the Swiss chard in an ovenproof pot with a cover. Place on the grill and cook for 35 to 40 minutes. Remove the cover and stir in slightly wet Swiss chard leaves; cook for 2 minutes, stir, and serve.

Baked Barbecue Beans

Makes 4 servings

Let's be realistic. Although they're delicious, most people are not going to cook baked beans from scratch. This version begins with canned baked beans, but within 15 to 20 minutes, they come out tasting like something special. They're particularly good with grilled pork chops or beef ribs.

Grill temperature

medium, then low

One 12-ounce can baked beans, drained

2 tablespoons molasses

2 tablespoons honey

2 tablespoons catsup

2 tablespoons brown sugar

½ teaspoon Tabasco sauce

¼ teaspoon Worcestershire sauce

Salt and pepper to taste

Place all of the ingredients in an ovenproof pot with a cover. Place the pot on the grill on medium heat, and when the beans come to a simmer, reduce heat to low or more to cooler edge of grill. Cook for 15 to 20 minutes.

Roasted
Chinese Eggplant

Makes 6 side-dish servings or 2 luncheon entrees with rice

Pacific Rim cooking is usually done in a wok, and wok cooking works well on a grill because of the high heat. The result here is eggplant that is crispy outside and soft inside. Regular eggplant can be substituted for the long, light-purple Chinese variety, but the results may not be as moist. If this is the case, add more wine. Hoisin sauce is a Chinese barbecue sauce sold in most supermarkets. If unavailable, substitute equal amounts of catsup and soy sauce or add soy sauce to molasses-based barbecue sauce.

3 Chinese eggplants

¼ cup vegetable oil

I medium white onion, cut into I-inch dice

½ cup finely diced scallion

½ tablespoon chopped fresh ginger

4 cloves garlic, sliced

¼ cup hoisin sauce

I cup white wine

Rub the eggplants with oil and grill them until slightly brown, turning them several times. Cut the eggplants into 2-inch cubes. Place in a nonstick skillet or black cast-iron skillet and add the remaining ingredients. Place the pan on the grill and cook, stirring frequently, until the vegetables are tender, about 10 minutes.

120

Grilling
with
Chef
George
Hirsch

Grilled Marinated
Vegetables

Makes 4 to 6 servings

These vegetables can be used in so many ways. Arrange them on whole-grain bread spread with Dijon mustard as a summer snack, slice and use on pizza, or chop and combine with pasta. Marinating the vegetables before grilling will make them caramelize better and be more flavorful.

**Grill
temperature**

high

> **4 zucchini, cut lengthwise into ¼-inch slices**
>
> **I large eggplant, peeled and cut lengthwise into ¼-inch slices**
>
> **2 large red onions, sliced into disks but not separated**
>
> **8 large, firm mushrooms**
>
> **I recipe Thyme-and-Lemon Marinade (page 149)**

Place the vegetables in the marinade and let them sit for 1 hour at room temperature. Remove the vegetables from the marinade and grill, turning frequently, for 8 to 10 minutes.

Spaghetti Squash Alfredo

Makes 4 appetizer servings or 8 side-dish servings

Grill temperature

medium, then high

Spaghetti squash is a hard, yellow, football-shape squash, and a fall favorite. Once you steam it and scrape out the innards, you have something reminiscent of thin spaghetti. These "noodles" can be substituted in almost any type of spaghetti recipe with tomato sauce. They can even be tossed with prosciutto or given the "Alfredo treatment." While many of us are trying to cook lower-fat fare, sometimes we have to let ourselves go—thus the cream in this dish. For a thinner consistency, omit the egg yolks. The cooked squash strands can also be tossed with butter and honey and served with roast Cornish hens or a pork roast.

1 spaghetti squash

4 tablespoons (½ stick) butter, melted

1 cup heavy cream

½ cup finely shredded Fontina cheese

¼ cup grated Parmesan cheese

2 egg yolks

Finely ground black pepper to taste

Pinch ground nutmeg

122

Grilling
with
Chef
George
Hirsch

Slice the squash in half lengthwise and brush the cut sides with 2 tablespoons of the butter. Cover the squash with foil and place, foil side down, on the grill for 25 minutes, or until tender. Remove the squash and allow it to cool slightly. Scrape out the "spaghetti" from the squash with a large fork and place it in a black cast-iron skillet. Add the remaining 2 tablespoons of butter, cream, Fontina, Parmesan, egg yolks, pepper, and nutmeg, and toss lightly.

Place the skillet on the grill on high and cook until the mixture bubbles. Serve immediately.

Baked Potatoes
with Gorgonzola Stuffing

Makes 6 servings

Grill temperature

medium-high

Ten years ago few people outside of the Northeast and a few large cities had ever heard of Gorgonzola, an Italian blue-veined cheese. It still can be hard to find, and if that's the case in your area, Cheddar, Fontina, or a good Swiss can be substituted. This dish works well for entertaining because the potatoes can be cooked ahead of time and stored in the refrigerator, then finished off at the last minute.

6 large baking potatoes, washed

¼ cup vegetable oil

½ cup crumbled Gorgonzola cheese

¼ cup chopped walnuts

2 tablespoons chopped chives

Ground black pepper to taste

¼ teaspoon Tabasco sauce

I cup plain yogurt

Rub the potatoes with oil and wrap each one in foil. Place on the grill and cook for 30 to 40 minutes. Test for doneness by inserting a sharp knife in the center of a potato. It should go in easily. Remove the potatoes from the grill and cool.

Remove the foil and slice the potatoes lengthwise, ¼ inch from the top. Scoop out the pulp, leaving a ¼-inch shell. Mash the pulp and place it in a bowl with

124

Grilling
with
Chef
George
Hirsch

the remaining ingredients. Place the potatoes in a pan and place the pan on the grill over medium-high heat. Cook for 5 to 8 minutes, or until hot.

Ratatouille

Makes 4 servings

Ratatouille is as versatile as its name is long. Serve it as a side dish, hot or at room temperature, or with rice or pasta. At breakfast, top a poached egg with ratatouille or fold some into an omelet.

Grill temperature

medium

2 bell peppers, cut into ½-inch dice

1 medium zucchini, sliced

4 plum tomatoes, quartered

1 onion, cut into ½-inch dice

4 cloves Caramelized Garlic (page 111)

¼ cup olive oil

¼ cup dry white wine

¼ teaspoon Tabasco sauce

¼ teaspoon dried thyme

¼ teaspoon dried basil

Salt and pepper to taste

In a nonstick or black cast-iron skillet, combine all of the ingredients. Cover and cook on the grill for 10 minutes. Remove the cover, stir, replace the cover, and cook for 10 minutes longer. Serve hot or at room temperature.

Mickey's Eggplant-and-Garlic Relish

Each jar makes 4 to 6 servings as a vegetable accompaniment

This recipe is from my mother-in-law, Michelina Rotella, and has always been a favorite in our family around the holidays. The bitter eggplant and vinegar relish make an excellent contrast to squid, baccalà, smoked fish or any strong, salty seafood. Of course, you'll need two or three loaves of Italian bread for mopping up the juices. You'll also need two sterilized glass quart jars for storing the relish in the refrigerator.

2 to 3 small eggplants

1 head garlic

Kosher salt

2 to 3 ribs celery, cut into ½-inch dice

½ cup red-wine vinegar

1 ½ cups white distilled vinegar

1 teaspoon dried oregano

Peel the eggplants and cut them into ¼- by ¼- by 1-inch fingers. Separate the garlic into cloves, but do not peel.

To remove excess moisture from the eggplant, sprinkle it with salt and place in a colander. Cover with a plate, place a heavy weight, such as a can of tomatoes, on top, and let it sit for about an hour. (Remove the plate and weight every 15 minutes and stir the eggplant.)

Layer the eggplant, garlic, and celery in the clean glass jars. Combine the vinegars and oregano in a separate measuring cup and pour over the vegetables, up to the tops of the bottles. Cover tightly and turn upside down to remove excess air. Invert and store for 1 month before using.

Tex-Mex New Potatoes

Makes 6 servings

In this recipe, the potatoes are cooked in a "pouch" of aluminum foil. The outer skins that touch the foil become caramelized and crusty. For an extra twist, top the potatoes with shredded Monterey Jack cheese or your favorite chili.

Grill temperature

medium-high

3 cups thinly sliced new red potatoes

¼ cup (½ stick) butter, cut into bits

I whole head Caramelized Garlic (page I I I), skinned

½ tablespoon ground cumin

¼ teaspoon Tabasco sauce

¼ teaspoon Worcestershire sauce

¼ tablespoon finely chopped scallion

¼ cup finely chopped red bell pepper

Large piece heavy-duty foil

Combine all of the ingredients and place in the center of the piece of foil. Fold into a square pouch and place on the grill. Cook, turning every 10 minutes, for a total of 35 to 40 minutes.

Stuffed Jalapeños

Grill temperature

high

At a flea market in California, I came across some locally grown jalapeño peppers that were outstanding. I had never seen anything like them on the East Coast. At 25 cents a pound, I went a little crazy and bought about 25 pounds to bring back to the restaurant. We began scratching our heads, wondering what we were going to do with them, and figured we could always add them to all the staff meals. Finally, we came up with Stuffed Jalapeños. After all, we reasoned, if you can stuff a bell pepper, why not a jalapeño? Because the seeds are removed, they are not fiery hot but still have a little bit of a kick. The cheese makes them nice and creamy on the inside, and the cornmeal adds crispness to the outside.

¼ **cup cream cheese**

¼ **cup shredded Cheddar cheese**

2 **tablespoons chopped scallion**

1 **teaspoon finely chopped cilantro**

Salt and pepper to taste

16 **jalapeño peppers**

2 **tablespoons bread crumbs**

¼ **cup fine cornmeal or** *masa harina*

Combine the cream cheese, Cheddar, scallion, cilantro, salt, and pepper in a bowl and mix well.

Grill the jalapeños for about 3 to 4 minutes, turning them frequently. Slice them lengthwise from tip to stem, but do not cut them in half. Carefully remove the seeds. Place the stuffing inside, and reshape the peppers to their original form. Place the peppers in a nonstick pan, sprinkle them with cornmeal, and heat for 5 to 6 minutes, or until hot, on the grill or stovetop.

Apple Sauerkraut

Makes 6 to 8 servings

Very few cooks have the gumption to make sauerkraut at home. It takes 4 to 6 weeks of brining, skimming, and pressing the cabbage down to make sure it's covered with brine. Most would rather make a quick run to the grocer. Apple sauerkraut takes that horrible can of prepared sauerkraut you buy in the supermarket and transforms it into a wonderful side dish for grilled pork, sausages, or even the all-American hot dog. If you can buy sauerkraut in a plastic bag at the deli or refrigerator section, by all means do so. In either case, be sure to rinse it well to get rid of the excess salt and vinegar. What's nice about this recipe is that if you don't have one of the ingredients, such as caraway seeds, it won't be a catastrophe. And it doesn't really matter if you use white vinegar instead of cider vinegar. Anything you add to store-bought sauerkraut is an improvement.

Grill temperature

low

129

Vegetables

(continued)

4 strips bacon, coarsely chopped

1 small onion, sliced

2 green apples, such as Granny Smith

½ cup chicken stock

¼ cup dry white wine

2 tablespoons cider vinegar

2 tablespoons light brown sugar

1 teaspoon caraway seeds

1 potato, peeled and finely grated

4 cups sauerkraut, rinsed and drained

Heat the bacon, onion, and apple in a nonstick skillet or black cast-iron skillet on the grill until the bacon begins to crisp. Drain off any excess bacon fat, add the remaining ingredients, and mix well. Cover and cook for 20 minutes, or until the potato is tender.

Lentil Compote

Makes 6 servings

This is the sort of dish you think about serving on that first cool, crisp fall evening. It's also a good choice for a tailgate party, along with grilled salmon or shrimp and smoked meats and sausage.

½ pound lentils

2 tablespoons olive oil

I small onion, diced fine

2 ribs celery, diced fine

I small green bell pepper, diced fine

I cup cooked corn niblets

2 tablespoons chopped cilantro

I tablespoon chopped fresh basil

I cup chicken stock

Salt and pepper to taste

Place the lentils in a saucepan and cover them with 3 cups of water. Bring to a boil on grill or stovetop, lower the heat, and cook until the lentils are tender, about 20 minutes.

Combine the olive oil, onion, celery, and green pepper in a nonstick skillet or black cast-iron skillet, and place it on the grill. Cook, stirring frequently, until the vegetables are tender. Stir in the lentils, corn, cilantro, basil, and stock. Season with salt and pepper. Serve warm.

Grill
Temperature

medium-low

Red Beans and Rice

Makes 6 to 8 servings

Red beans and rice is a southern Louisiana specialty. It was traditionally cooked on Monday using the leftover ham bone from Sunday's dinner, so make sure you add a ham bone if you happen to have one hanging around. On the other hand, leave out the meat and you have a vegetarian version.

1 pound dry kidney beans

2 tablespoons olive oil

¼ cup finely chopped bacon

1 cup chopped scallion

1 cup chopped celery

1 medium onion, chopped

3 cloves garlic, chopped

¼ cup diced smoked ham

1 pound smoked sausage, sliced

6 cups chicken stock, vegetable stock, or water

2 bay leaves

1 teaspoon Tabasco sauce

½ teaspoon Worcestershire sauce

Salt and pepper to taste

3 cups hot cooked rice

132

Grilling
with
Chef
George
Hirsch

Soak the beans in 6 cups of water for 8 hours or overnight.

Place a large iron pot on the grill or over charcoal. Add the olive oil and bacon and cook for 1 to 2 minutes. Add the scallion, celery, onion, and garlic, and cook until the onion is transparent, stirring occasionally.

Drain the beans and discard the soaking liquid. Add the beans, ham, sausage, chicken stock, bay leaves, Tabasco, and Worcestershire sauce to the vegetable mixture. Cook for 45 minutes, or until the beans are creamy, adding additional liquid if necessary. Discard bay leaves. Season with salt and pepper. Serve over rice.

Mock Dirty Rice

Makes 6 to 8 servings

Grill temperature

medium

This version of dirty rice breaks tradition with that well-known Louisiana dish that calls for chicken livers. We've found, at buffets, that once someone finds out that a dish has chicken livers in it, the word spreads, and everyone walks right by it. So, we've substituted ground beef. You get the same look and consistency, but the taste isn't as sharp. Purists can go back and add chicken livers if they wish.

1 pound ground beef

1 cup half-and-half

1 cup finely chopped mushrooms

1 cup water or chicken stock

1 small green bell pepper, chopped fine

1 small onion, chopped

½ cup finely chopped scallion

2 ribs celery, diced fine

6 cloves Caramelized Garlic (page 111)

2 bay leaves

¼ teaspoon Tabasco sauce

¼ teaspoon dried thyme

¼ teaspoon dried oregano

Salt and pepper to taste

1 cup uncooked rice

134

Grilling
with
Chef
George
Hirsch

In a black cast-iron skillet, brown the beef slightly on the grill, breaking it apart as it begins to cook. Add the remaining ingredients, except the rice, and stir well. Add the rice, mix well, cover, and cook for 40 minutes, or until the rice is tender. Remove the bay leaves and serve.

Vegetable Kabobs

Everybody likes to serve kabobs because they look so good and are so easy to prepare. There is no one recipe; the cook should be creative and use what's fresh in the marketplace. When you purchase metal skewers, look for flat ones. Then, when you turn the kabobs, the food will turn over and not roll around, as it would on a round skewer. When using wooden skewers, presoak them for 30 minutes in water to keep them from burning on the grill. Marinating the vegetables in a high-sugar marinade will help them caramelize.

Grill
temperature

medium-low

(continued)

Cherry tomatoes

Green bell peppers, cut into 1-inch squares

Mushrooms caps

Fresh pineapple, cut into 1-inch chunks

Pineapple-Ginger Marinade

2 cups pineapple juice

2 tablespoons finely chopped fresh ginger

3 tablespoons honey

2 tablespoons brown sugar

1 tablespoon finely chopped fresh cilantro

1 tablespoon soy sauce

¼ teaspoon Tabasco sauce

Hollowed-out pineapple halves

Hot cooked rice

Shredded coconut

Using flat metal skewers, thread the cherry tomatoes, green pepper, mushroom caps, and pineapple. In a nonreactive bowl, combine all of the marinade ingredients and mix well. Marinate the kabobs for 1 hour in the marinade at room temperature.

Grill the kabobs for 15 to 20 minutes, basting occasionally with the marinade. Fill the pineapple shells with hot cooked rice and lay the kabobs on top. Sprinkle with coconut.

Vegetable Burger

Makes 4 to 6 burgers

This burger may be meatless, but it's extremely flavorful because of the oats, beans, and nuts. Try it on a whole-wheat bun with a grainy mustard.

One 16- or 19-ounce can cannellini beans, drained and mashed

2 tablespoons uncooked oatmeal

One 10-ounce package frozen chopped spinach, thawed and squeezed dry

1 cup fresh bread crumbs

½ cup finely chopped cooked carrot

½ cup finely chopped pecans

¼ cup finely chopped red bell pepper

¼ cup mayonnaise or yogurt

2 tablespoons chopped scallion

1 tablespoon chopped fresh parsley or cilantro

¼ teaspoon Tabasco sauce

¼ teaspoon Worcestershire sauce

Salt and pepper to taste

2 tablespoons olive oil

4 to 6 whole-wheat buns

In a large bowl, combine all of the ingredients except the olive oil and buns. Shape the mixture into four to six burgers, pressing firmly. Chill for 2 hours. Before grilling, brush the burgers with olive oil. Grill for 4 to 5 minutes on each side, turning only once. Serve on whole-wheat buns.

Tropical Fruit Relish

Makes 6 servings

The first time I had green papaya relish, I thought it was kind of crazy to use unripened fruit, but I found it is not uncommon in Caribbean, Hawaiian, and Thai cuisines. This relish has a very refreshing flavor, and it goes well with fish from Caribbean and Pacific waters—a perfect example of combining local fish with local fruit. Serve this with grilled swordfish, mahimahi, or grouper.

1 large half-ripened papaya

2 mangoes, diced

1 avocado, diced

1 red bell pepper, diced

Juice of 3 limes

Red pepper flakes to taste

3 tablespoons blanched and chopped fresh mint

2 tablespoons chopped cilantro

Peel the papaya, discard the seeds, and cut into ¼-inch dice. Peel the mangoes, cut the flesh away from the stones, and cut into ¼-inch dice. Peel the avocado, remove the pit, and cut into ¼-inch dice.

In a nonreactive bowl, combine the chopped fruit with the remaining ingredients. Toss gently and serve at room temperature.

Sauces, Dressings, and Marinades

∙∙

Before using a vinaigrette or oil-based marinade or salad dressing, leave it out at room temperature for a few hours to improve its flavor. If you're using a mayonnaise-type dressing, the flavor will improve if it's made a day ahead, but the dressing must be kept chilled at all times.

Santa Cruz
Caesar Dressing

Makes about 2 ½ cups

6 cloves garlic

4 anchovy fillets (optional)

Juice of ½ lemon

2 cups mayonnaise (homemade or commercial)

2 tablespoons grated Parmesan cheese

½ teaspoon ground cumin

1 tablespoon chopped cilantro

¼ teaspoon Tabasco sauce

¼ teaspoon dry mustard

¼ teaspoon Worcestershire sauce

4 ounces plain yogurt

Combine the garlic, anchovy fillets, and lemon juice in a food processor or blender, and process until smooth. Add the mayonnaise, Parmesan cheese, cumin, cilantro, Tabasco, mustard, and Worcestershire sauce. Process for 30 to 40 seconds, or until well blended. Remove and place the mixture in a bowl. Stir in the yogurt and refrigerate. The dressing can be thinned out, if necessary, with a few drops of cold water.

Sesame Dressing

I cup vegetable oil

⅓ cup cider vinegar

½ cup soy sauce

2 tablespoons honey

2 tablespoons water

I tablespoon toasted sesame seeds

I tablespoon sesame oil

2 cloves garlic, chopped fine

2 tablespoons finely chopped scallion

I tablespoon finely chopped fresh ginger

Combine all of the ingredients in a jar with a tight-fitting lid and shake well.

Honey-Poppy
Vinaigrette

Makes 1 cup

½ **cup vegetable oil**

2 tablespoons cider vinegar

2 tablespoons white distilled vinegar

2 tablespoons honey

2 tablespoons toasted poppy seeds

¼ **teaspoon dry mustard**

¼ **teaspoon Tabasco sauce**

Combine all of the ingredients in a small bowl and whisk until well blended. Allow the flavors to meld for 1 hour at room temperature before using. This dressing will keep indefinitely stored tightly covered in the refrigerator.

142

Grilling
with
Chef
George
Hirsch

Hazelnut Dressing

Makes about 1 cup

½ cup vegetable oil

3 tablespoons cider vinegar

1 tablespoon brown sugar

Salt and pepper to taste

1 green apple, cored and diced

¼ cup hazelnuts, toasted and chopped

Combine the oil, vinegar, sugar, salt, and pepper in a small bowl and whisk until smooth. Stir in the apple and hazelnuts.

Yogurt Dressing

Makes about 1 cup

¾ cup plain yogurt

¼ cup sour cream

1 tablespoon honey

1 tablespoon chopped scallion

¼ teaspoon coriander

In a small bowl, combine all of the ingredients and mix well.

Grilling Vinaigrette

Makes about 1 cup

Although this "grilling vinaigrette" can be used to marinate vegetables before grilling, it also makes a delicious dressing over salad greens.

> ¾ cup olive oil
>
> 1 tablespoon Dijon mustard
>
> ¼ teaspoon Tabasco sauce
>
> 1 teaspoon dried parsley
>
> 1 teaspoon dried basil
>
> 1 teaspoon dried thyme
>
> 2 cloves Caramelized Garlic (page 111)
>
> Salt and pepper to taste
>
> Juice of ½ lemon
>
> 1 tablespoon balsamic vinegar
>
> 1 tablespoon dry white wine

Combine the oil, mustard, Tabasco, parsley, basil, thyme, garlic, salt, and pepper in a small bowl, and whisk until well blended. Drizzle in the lemon juice, vinegar, and wine, and mix well. Allow the vinaigrette to sit at room temperature for a day to improve its flavor.

144

Grilling
with
Chef
George
Hirsch

Dijon-Horseradish
Dressing

Makes 1 cup

Here's a versatile dressing that is easily assembled from ingredients most of us have in the refrigerator. It goes especially well on grilled beef and poultry. You can also use it as a dip for crudités.

½ **cup sour cream**

½ **cup mayonnaise**

2 tablespoons Dijon mustard

1 tablespoon horseradish

2 tablespoons finely chopped scallion

Juice of ½ **lemon**

Combine all of the ingredients in a small bowl and mix well. Chill for 1 hour.

Tomato-Gorgonzola Dressing

Makes about 3 cups

4 ounces Gorgonzola cheese, softened

1 cup mayonnaise (homemade or commercial)

1 cup plain yogurt

2 tablespoons catsup

2 tablespoons white distilled vinegar

2 cloves garlic, chopped fine

1/4 teaspoon dried basil

1/4 teaspoon dried thyme

1/4 teaspoon dried parsley

1/4 teaspoon Tabasco sauce

1/4 teaspoon Worcestershire sauce

Combine all of the ingredients in a small bowl and mix well. Chill for 2 hours before using.

146

Grilling
with
Chef
George
Hirsch

Marinade for Steak

Makes about 1 ¼ cups

¼ **cup olive oil**

2 **tablespoons balsamic vinegar**

¼ **cup cane syrup or dark corn syrup**

4 **cloves garlic, sliced**

1 **teaspoon Worcestershire sauce**

¼ **teaspoon Tabasco sauce**

1 **tablespoon crushed peppercorns**

Salt to taste

Combine all of the ingredients in a small bowl and mix well.

Southwest Marinade

Makes about 1 cup

½ **cup olive oil**

¼ **cup dry white wine**

Juice and zest of 1 lime

2 **tablespoons chopped cilantro**

¼ **teaspoon Tabasco sauce**

4 **cloves garlic, chopped**

2 **tablespoons honey**

Combine all of the ingredients in a small bowl and mix well.

Pacific Rim
Marinade

This versatile marinade can be used with all kinds of poultry and many seafood recipes. Its zesty taste is a combination of acidic, pungent, spicy, and salty flavors.

2 fresh limes

½ cup olive oil

3 tablespoons sesame oil

I tablespoon soy sauce

2 tablespoons grated fresh ginger

¼ teaspoon Tabasco sauce

I teaspoon finely chopped cilantro

Cut the zest from the limes. Place the limes on a cutting board and firmly press and roll them back and forth with the palm of your hand to loosen the juice. Cut the limes in half and squeeze out the juice. In a small bowl, combine the lime juice with the remaining ingredients and mix well.

148

Grilling
with
Chef
George
Hirsch

Thyme-and-Lemon Marinade

Makes 1 cup

¾ cup olive oil

¼ cup fresh lemon juice

1 tablespoon dried thyme

½ teaspoon sugar

Salt and pepper to taste

Combine all of the ingredients in a bowl and mix well. Prepare this marinade a day before using for best flavor.

Porterhouse Marinade

Makes ⅓ cup

¼ cup olive oil

2 tablespoons steak sauce

1 teaspoon Tabasco sauce

1 teaspoon Worcestershire sauce

3 cloves garlic, minced

Combine all of the ingredients in a small bowl and mix well.

Teriyaki Marinade

Makes about 2 ½ cups

This marinade is as good with chicken as it is with beef, pork, fish, and even chicken livers. Because their flavors are so prominent in the marinade, use high-quality soy sauce and sesame oil. The larger the piece of meat, the longer it takes to marinate. Chicken breasts and fish require only 30 minutes of marinating, while a whole chicken or large pieces of beef may take up to several hours.

½ cup vegetable oil

½ cup soy sauce

¼ cup sherry or sweet white wine

2 tablespoons honey

1 tablespoon sesame oil

1 tablespoon finely chopped fresh ginger

1 tablespoon white distilled vinegar

1 tablespoon sesame seeds

2 cloves garlic, chopped fine

Combine all of the ingredients in a nonreactive bowl and mix well.

150

Grilling
with
Chef
George
Hirsch

Savory Bourbon Sauce

Makes about I cup

Serve this sauce with steak.

¼ **cup Dijon mustard**

¼ **cup steak sauce**

¼ **cup bourbon**

¼ **cup honey**

Juice of I lemon

In a small saucepan, combine all of the ingredients and heat until warm.

Honey Pork Sauce

Makes I ¾ cups

I **cup catsup**

½ **cup honey**

¼ **cup Madeira or other sweet wine**

2 **tablespoons cider vinegar**

½ **teaspoon Worcestershire sauce**

In a small bowl, combine all of the ingredients and mix well.

Pork Barbecue Sauce

Makes about 3 cups

To add a hickory flavor to this sauce, place the sauce in a deep foil container and cover with foil. Cut a few slits in the top and place the container in a smoker for about an hour.

2 strips bacon, chopped

½ cup chopped onion

½ cup chopped scallion

½ cup cider vinegar

¼ cup brown sugar

¼ cup granulated sugar

1 cup catsup

1 cup chili sauce

½ tablespoon Worcestershire sauce

½ teaspoon Tabasco sauce

½ teaspoon ground cumin

In a heavy skillet, cook the bacon. When it begins to give off fat, add the onion and scallion, and cook until the onion is transparent. (If the bacon is very lean, add a tablespoon of vegetable oil.) Stir in the vinegar, sugars, and catsup. Bring to a boil, lower the heat, and simmer for 5 minutes. Stir in the chili sauce, Worcestershire sauce, Tabasco, and cumin, and simmer 10 minutes longer.

152

Grilling
with
Chef
George
Hirsch

Sweet Pork Sauce

Makes 1 ½ cups

1 cup catsup

½ cup honey

1 tablespoon soy sauce

1 teaspoon finely chopped fresh ginger

Juice of 1 lemon

¼ teaspoon Tabasco sauce

In a small bowl, combine all of the ingredients and mix well.

Chicken or
Rib Barbecue Sauce

Makes about 2 cups

Any sauce that contains a lot of sugar—and this one does in the hoisin, catsup, and honey—should be brushed on the meat during the last minutes of cooking, because the high heat from the grill can burn the sugar, and you'll wind up with a charred slab instead of a tasty morsel.

½ **cup catsup**

½ **cup chili sauce**

¼ **cup soy sauce**

¼ **cup hoisin sauce**

¼ **cup honey**

I **tablespoon sesame oil**

4 **to 5 cloves garlic, chopped fine**

¼ **cup finely chopped scallion**

2 **tablespoons cider vinegar**

I **teaspoon Worcestershire sauce**

In a medium bowl, combine all of the ingredients and mix well. To use: Season chicken pieces or ribs with a dry rub (recipes follow). Cook on a medium-hot grill for 25 to 30 minutes. Brush with barbecue sauce and continue cooking the meat for another 10 to 15 minutes, turning every 5 minutes and basting frequently with sauce.

Chicken Dry Rub

Makes about ½ cup

A rub is a highly flavored dry powder that is rubbed on fairly tender meats, such as chicken, or on a tough piece of meat, like a brisket, which is cooked for a long time at a low temperature. Marinades, on the other hand, are used for preservation and tenderizing.

¼ **cup paprika**

½ **teaspoon cayenne**

1 tablespoon black pepper

1 teaspoon ground nutmeg

1 teaspoon garlic powder

1 tablespoon sugar

Combine all of the ingredients in a small bowl. To use: Rub the mixture on all sides of the chicken and refrigerate for 2 to 3 hours before grilling.

Pork Dry Rub

Makes about ¾ cup

This is not a marinade and will not tenderize the meat, but it will enhance its flavor. It can be made in advance and stored in a jar with a tight-fitting lid. Never add salt to a rub because it will draw out the meat juices.

¼ **cup paprika**

2 **tablespoons dried thyme**

2 **tablespoons dried rosemary**

2 **tablespoons garlic powder**

½ **teaspoon ground black pepper**

½ **teaspoon ground nutmeg**

¼ **teaspoon cayenne**

In a small bowl, combine all of the ingredients and mix well. To use: Rub the mixture on all sides of the pork and refrigerate for 2 to 3 hours before grilling.

Pork Baste

Makes about ½ cup

¼ cup (½ stick) margarine, melted

¼ cup fresh lemon juice

Zest of 1 lemon

1 teaspoon Worcestershire sauce

½ teaspoon Tabasco sauce

½ teaspoon paprika

Freshly ground black pepper to taste

In a bowl, combine all of the ingredients and mix well.

Milk Marinade
for Seafood

Makes 2 cups

Use this marinade when you want to tone down the flavor of strong tasting fish such as bluefish, mako, or mackerel. Or use it for dipping fish fillets before coating them with flour, bread crumbs, or cornmeal.

> **2 cups milk**
>
> **3 cloves garlic, chopped**
>
> **¼ teaspoon dried thyme**
>
> **¼ teaspoon dried basil**
>
> **¼ teaspoon ground nutmeg**
>
> **¼ teaspoon Tabasco sauce**
>
> **¼ teaspoon Worcestershire sauce**

Combine all of the ingredients in a jar and keep refrigerated. To use: Marinate fish for 30 minutes.

Grilling
with
Chef
George
Hirsch

Rémoulade

Makes 2 cups

This is a very flavorful, highly seasoned dressing with French origins and is particularly popular in Creole cooking. Use it as a dip for shrimp or as a salad dressing.

> 1 cup olive oil
>
> ½ cup Dijon mustard
>
> ⅓ cup vinegar (half red, half white)
>
> ¼ cup chopped scallion
>
> 4 cloves Caramelized Garlic (page 111), crushed
>
> 1 tablespoon paprika
>
> 1 tablespoon capers
>
> 1 tablespoon chopped fresh Italian parsley
>
> ¼ teaspoon Tabasco sauce

Whisk the olive oil and mustard in a medium bowl. Stir in the vinegar a few drops at a time. Stir in the remaining ingredients. Refrigerate for several hours to improve the flavor.

Texas Barbecue Sauce

Makes about 3 cups

I cup canned beef bouillon

¼ cup catsup

¼ cup cider vinegar

I cup fresh or canned whole plum tomatoes, chopped

¼ cup brown sugar

¼ cup diced white onion

½ teaspoon Worcestershire sauce

¼ teaspoon Tabasco sauce

In a nonreactive saucepan, combine all the ingredients and simmer 4 to 5 minutes. Serve warm over brisket.

160

Grilling
with
Chef
George
Hirsch

Beef

· ·

When cooking beef, always start with a strong, hot fire. If you want to make crosshatch marks on the steaks, reposition them only once—don't keep turning them over. If you do, they will start to cool, and the meat will steam instead of getting a nice caramelized look on the outside. Never salt the steak before grilling because it draws out the juices, and don't salt the meat until after you've tasted it. Marinated meats seldom require any additional seasoning.

Never stab meat with a fork or you will lose the juices. One of the most common grilling problems is knowing when the meat is done to your liking. The worst thing you can do is to cut off a piece. The best method to judge doneness is by touch. Press the steak with your finger (it won't be that hot), and if it feels firm, the steak is well done; if it feels slightly resistant, the steak is medium; and if it's spongy, the steak is rare to medium-rare.

Grilled
Seven-Bone Steak

Makes 4 servings

Seven-bone steak, or chuck steak, is one of the most economical of all beef steaks and one of the tastiest. The marinade doesn't really tenderize the steak, but it does enhance the flavor. Trim the fat to about ¼ inch and make small cuts in the fat with a sharp knife to prevent the steak from curling up on the grill.

> 6 cloves garlic, sliced
>
> 2 teaspoons Tabasco sauce
>
> 2 teaspoons soy sauce
>
> 2 teaspoons freshly ground black pepper
>
> 2 tablespoons olive oil
>
> 2 seven-bone blade steaks or cross-cut chuck steaks, about 1 ½ pounds each with bone
>
> 1 recipe Olive Relish (recipe follows)

Combine the garlic, Tabasco, soy sauce, pepper, and olive oil in a small bowl. Rub the mixture onto both sides of the steaks, and marinate for an hour or two in the refrigerator. Place the steaks on a hot grill for 1 minute. Using tongs, turn the steaks 45 degrees to make a crosshatch mark. Cook for 2 to 3 minutes more, and turn the steaks over. Move the steaks to a cooler edge of the grill, or raise the cooking grid, or lower the heat to medium, and cook until done. Avoid turning the steaks from side to side.

162

Grilling
with
Chef
George
Hirsch

Olive Relish

½ cup green olives, pitted and chopped

½ cup plum tomatoes, seeded and chopped

1 tablespoon chopped fresh basil

2 to 4 jalapeño peppers, seeded and chopped

Juice of 1 lemon

Salt and pepper to taste

In a small bowl, combine all of the ingredients and mix well.

Rib-eye Steak

Makes 4 servings

Rib-eye steaks are a bit fatty, which means, on the one hand, that they will be very flavorful, but, on the other hand, that you will have to be somewhat cautious, because more fat means a greater chance of a flare-up on the grill. Trim the steaks, leaving only ¼ inch of fat around the edges.

The steak marinade is definitely a flavor enhancer, and served with grilled Bermuda onions and grilled jalapeño peppers, these steaks are hard to resist.

> **Four 10- to 12-ounce boneless and tailless rib steaks**
>
> **1 recipe Marinade for Steak (page 147)**
>
> **2 tablespoons chopped fresh chives or scallion**

Brush both sides of the steaks with the marinade and refrigerate them for 24 hours.

Place the steaks on the grill over high heat. After 1 minute, lift the steaks, using tongs, and turn them 45 degrees to make a crosshatch mark. After 2 to 3 minutes, turn the steaks and move them to the cooler edges of the grill, or raise the cooking grid, or lower the heat to medium. Continue cooking until the meat is done. Avoid turning the steaks over several times. Sprinkle the steaks with chives before serving.

164

Grilling
with
Chef
George
Hirsch

New York Strip
Sirloin Steak

Makes 4 servings

This is an expensive piece of meat, and you don't want to overcook it. For a fabulous meal, serve the steak with Grilled Portobello Mushrooms and Dijon-Horseradish Dressing.

Grill temperature

high, then medium

Four 10- to 12-ounce boneless and tailless sirloin steaks, trimmed,

with ¼ inch of fat remaining

1 recipe Marinade for Steak (page 147)

Brush both sides of the steaks with the marinade and refrigerate them for 1 to 2 days. Place the steaks on a hot grill for 1 minute. Using tongs, lift the steaks and turn them 45 degrees to make crosshatch marks. After 2 to 3 minutes, turn the steaks over and move them to the cooler edges of the grill, or raise the cooking grid, or lower the heat to medium. Continue cooking until the meat is done. Don't turn the steaks over more than once.

Pinwheel Steak

Makes 4 servings

Grill temperature

high, then medium

Some butchers will sell pinwheel steaks already made, but it's easy enough to make them at home. Have your butcher cut full-size steaks from the round and not the smaller portion that is usually sold for London broil.

Two 1-pound round steaks

½ pound prosciutto or good-quality smoked ham, sliced thin

1 cup cooked spinach, drained

½ cup pine nuts or walnuts

8 fresh sage leaves

2 tablespoons grated Parmesan cheese

Freshly ground black pepper to taste

8 strips bacon, blanched

Olive oil

Cut off two pieces of plastic wrap double the size of the steaks. Place one piece on a cutting board and lay a round steak on top. Cover with the second sheet of plastic wrap. Using the flat side of a meat mallet, pound the meat until it becomes a long, flat sheet about ¼ inch thick. Do the same with the other steak.

Lay two long pieces of plastic wrap larger than the steaks on a flat surface, and lay one steak on each piece. Layer each steak with half the prosciutto, spinach, pine nuts, sage, and Parmesan, and season with pepper. Tightly roll up each steak, beginning with the long side. Roll the plastic wrap around the meat and twist the ends. Refrigerate until well chilled.

Unwrap the plastic, keeping the rolls intact. Roll four strips of bacon, evenly spaced, around each meat roll, and tie the center of the bacon with butcher's twine. Make three cuts between the slices of bacon to make four pinwheels from each roll.

Brush the pinwheels with olive oil, grill them for 2 minutes, and move them to the cooler edges of the grill, or raise the cooking grid or lower the heat to medium. Turn and cook to desired doneness, taking care not to overcook.

Sunday Braciole

Makes 4 servings

If you're out in the garden planting flowers in the early spring, or in the backyard raking leaves in the autumn, this is a good meal to put on the grill. It will be ready and waiting for hungry appetites.

Have your butcher slice the full width of the round and not the London-broil size. The sauce can also be served over rigatoni or ravioli.

Two 1-pound round steaks

1 cup cubed day-old French or Italian bread

½ cup milk

¼ cup raisins, plumped in boiling water to cover for 5 minutes

6 cloves Caramelized Garlic (page 111)

1 tablespoon chopped fresh sage

1 tablespoon grated Parmesan cheese

Freshly ground black pepper to taste

4 thin slices prosciutto

2 tablespoons olive oil

½ cup sliced onion

4 cloves garlic, sliced

¼ cup dry red wine

One 28-ounce can plum tomatoes, crushed (undrained)

1 tablespoon chopped fresh basil

Salt and pepper to taste

168

Grilling
with
Chef
George
Hirsch

Cut off two pieces of plastic wrap twice the size of the steaks. Lay one piece of plastic wrap on a flat surface or cutting board. Lay one of the steaks on top and cover with the second sheet of plastic wrap. With the flat side of a meat mallet, pound the steak until it is about ¼ inch thick. Do the same with the second steak.

In a medium bowl, combine the bread, milk, raisins, Caramelized Garlic, sage, Parmesan, and pepper. Spread half of the mixture evenly on each steak, and cover with slices of prosciutto. Beginning with the long side, roll each steak into a tight roll and tie securely with butcher's twine.

Brush the rolls with 1 tablespoon of olive oil and sear them on both sides on a hot grill. Heat a large cast-iron skillet on the grill and heat the remaining tablespoon of olive oil. Add the onion and garlic and cook for 2 minutes. Add the rolls to the pan and stir in the wine, tomato, basil, salt, and pepper. Bring to a simmer, cover, and cook gently over low heat for 1½ hours.

Texas Brisket with Chef George Hirsch's Seasoning Dust

Makes 10 to 12 servings

You can't come home from work and decide to make Texas brisket for dinner. It's simple to make, but it takes patience and slow cooking at a low temperature. If you cook it in a smoker, it will take from 8 to 9 hours at 195°F.; on the grill, it requires 5 to 6 hours.

The seasoning dust is rubbed into the meat, this is then aged for 3 to 5 days in the refrigerator. Don't cut off the excess fat from the brisket, because it will help baste the meat while it's cooking. An hour after the meat has finished cooking, cut off the fat, and the meat will almost fall apart.

¼ **cup sweet paprika**

2 **tablespoons garlic powder**

1 **tablespoon dried thyme**

1 **tablespoon dried basil**

1 **tablespoon dried oregano**

1 **tablespoon dried parsley**

1 **tablespoon coarsely ground black pepper**

½ **teaspoon cayenne**

½ **teaspoon ground nutmeg**

One 5-pound (or larger) fresh beef brisket

2 tablespoons Tabasco sauce

2 tablespoons Worcestershire sauce

1 recipe Texas Barbecue Sauce (page 160)

In a medium bowl, combine the paprika, garlic powder, thyme, basil, oregano, parsley, black pepper, cayenne, and nutmeg.

Dry the meat very well and rub it with the Tabasco and Worcestershire sauce. Cover the meat with ¼ inch of the seasoning dust on all sides. Place it in a bowl and loosely cover with foil. Refrigerate for 3 to 5 days. (The larger the piece of meat, the longer it will take for the seasonings to penetrate the flesh.)

Place the brisket on the grill for approximately 6 hours, with the fat side on top. (Or smoke the meat for 8 to 9 hours at 195°F. See smoking section, page 241.) Place a pan below the meat filled with water or other liquid to keep it moist and juicy. When the meat is cooked, take it off the grill and let it rest for 1 hour. Trim off the fat and slice the meat into thin pieces on an angle against the grain. Serve with Texas Barbecue Sauce.

Better Burger

Makes 4 to 6 servings

Burgers may have been the original reason why grills were invented. This one is a little fancier than most, because it's seasoned with garlic, scallions, mustard, Tabasco, and Worcestershire sauce.

The meat you choose makes a difference in the taste of the burger. The leanest meat doesn't necessarily make the best burger—you need some fat to keep it tender. When using any ground meat, keep it well chilled until cooking time.

> **2 pounds ground sirloin**
>
> **3 cloves Caramelized Garlic (page 111)**
>
> **2 tablespoons chopped scallion**
>
> **1 tablespoon Dijon mustard**
>
> **¼ teaspoon Tabasco sauce**
>
> **¼ teaspoon Worcestershire sauce**
>
> **Salt and freshly ground black pepper to taste**

In a medium bowl, combine all of the ingredients and mix with a fork, taking care not to overwork the meat. Divide the mixture into four to six equal portions and form into patties. Chill for 15 to 20 minutes. Place the burgers on the grill for 3 minutes. Turn and grill for 4 minutes for rare; 5 to 6 for medium.

172

Grilling
with
Chef
George
Hirsch

Sliced Porterhouse Steak with Peppercorns and Savory Bourbon Sauce

Makes 6 to 8 servings

Aporterhouse steak is a very expensive piece of meat that includes a nugget of the beef tenderloin.

Grill temperature

high

> **1 cup Porterhouse Marinade (page 149)**
>
> **4 tablespoons coarsely crushed peppercorns**
>
> **2 porterhouse steaks, cut 2 inches thick, 3 to 4 pounds total**
>
> **1 recipe Savory Bourbon Sauce (page 151)**

Combine the marinade and the peppercorns, and marinate the steaks in this mixture for 1 hour at room temperature or 3 to 4 hours in the refrigerator. If the steaks are refrigerated, allow them to return to room temperature before grilling. Cook the steaks for 4 to 5 minutes on each side for rare, turning only once. Remove the steaks from the grill and let them sit for 5 minutes on a warm platter before slicing. Serve with warm bourbon sauce.

Fish

. . . .

If you have cooked no other fish but salmon and swordfish on the grill, you're in for a surprise. Nothing lends itself better to grilling than seafood, and the list of possibilities is long. There are just a few basic principles to follow. First, use only the freshest fish and shellfish. If it doesn't smell good, it probably isn't. Fish should not smell like fish, it should smell like the sea. And, if grouper, for example, isn't available, don't give up on the recipe—substitute halibut, cod, mako, or tuna. Second, fish is very delicate, so don't flip it more than once, and always place it on a very hot grill so it doesn't end up steaming. Last, fish continues to cook after it has been taken off the grill, so be sure to take this into consideration when gauging doneness.

Garlic Mussels

Makes 4 servings

Mussels are inexpensive and easy to cook, but they're a chore to clean, unless you are lucky enough to have a fishmonger who carries farmed mussels (most of which come from the state of Maine). These mussels are free from mud and silt, but each still has a small beard, or bissop, that can be twisted off by hand or, if it's persistent, with pliers. Serve these mussels as an appetizer with lots of crusty bread for mopping up the juices, or boil up some pasta and heap them over it. Discard any open raw mussels or those that don't close when squeezed.

4 pounds mussels, cleaned and debearded

2 cups dry white wine

I head fresh garlic, peeled and coarsely chopped

¼ cup chopped fresh Italian parsley

I teaspoon red pepper flakes

¼ pound (I stick) butter, cut into small pieces

French or Italian bread

Place the mussels in a large stockpot. Add the wine, garlic, parsley, pepper flakes, and butter. Place the pot on the grill, cover, and cook for 6 to 8 minutes, shaking the pot a few times. Discard any mussels that do not open.

Remove the mussels from the cooking liquid and keep them warm. Boil the cooking liquid for 1 minute and strain it through cheesecloth. Pour the liquid into small bowls and use it for dipping the mussels. Serve with crusty French or Italian bread.

176

Grilling

with

Chef

George

Hirsch

Grilled Lobster
with Dijon Mustard

Makes 8 servings

Serve grilled lobster with Oyster Pie, or for a New England–style clambake, with Garlic Mussels, Montauk Indian Corn on the Cob, and boiled potatoes. If you have your lobsters split and cleaned at the fish store, grill them as soon as possible.

Grill temperature

high,
then medium

> 1 pound (4 sticks) unsalted butter, melted
>
> ½ cup Dijon mustard
>
> ¼ cup chopped fresh Italian parsley
>
> ¼ teaspoon Tabasco sauce
>
> Juice of 2 lemons
>
> Eight 1-pound lobsters, split and cleaned at your fish store

Combine the butter, mustard, parsley, Tabasco, and lemon juice in a medium bowl. Turn the lobsters over and brush the cavities and tail meat with the butter mixture. Place the lobsters on a hot grill, cavity sides down, and cook for 2 to 3 minutes on high. Turn the lobsters right-side up, brush again with the butter sauce, and move them to the cooler edges of the grill. Cook for 5 to 6 minutes. Serve with the remaining warm butter mixture.

Cioppino

Makes 4 servings

Grill temperature

medium, then low, then high

I once took this dish off the menu in my restaurant because I didn't have enough tureens for serving it. After looking around and finding that I couldn't buy any more of the ones I wanted, I came up with a new "tureen." We had extra round loaves of bread one night, so I hollowed out the centers and served the cioppino in them. As a result, cioppino in bread bowls became so popular, I never went back to look for the soup tureens.

In the New York area, when people see seafood and red sauce, they look underneath it for spaghetti, so we do serve linguine with the cioppino, but that's up to you. If round bread is not available, use soup bowls and serve warm sourdough bread on the side.

¼ cup olive oil

I large onion, chopped fine

8 cloves garlic, chopped fine

½ cup finely chopped scallion

½ cup finely chopped celery

I teaspoon chopped cilantro

2 bay leaves

I teaspoon dried basil

¼ teaspoon Tabasco sauce

I cup dry red wine

One 28-ounce can whole Italian plum tomatoes, crushed

178

Grilling
with
Chef
George
Hirsch

One 28-ounce can tomato puree

4 cups fish stock

4 small round loaves sourdough or Italian bread

½ cup olive oil

2 Dungeness crabs, cleaned and cracked, or 0 blue claw crabs

I pound medium shrimp (26 to 30 per pound)

I pound firm fish (such as halibut, mako, swordfish, or tuna)

I 2 littleneck clams (optional)

I pound mussels (optional)

In a large stockpot, heat the oil over medium heat on the grill or stovetop. Add the onion, garlic, scallion, and celery, and sauté for 3 minutes. Add the cilantro, bay leaves, basil, Tabasco, and red wine, and cook for 30 seconds. Stir in the plum tomatoes, puree, and fish stock; simmer for 15 minutes over low heat.

Hollow out the centers of the bread, making each an individual bowl. Lightly toast the bread on the grill. Lightly brush the crabs, shrimp, and fish with olive oil. Grill over high heat for 30 seconds. Add the grilled seafood to the cioppino sauce and cook for 5 to 6 minutes. Add the clams and mussels and simmer until their shells open, approximately 5 to 6 minutes longer. Discard the bay leaves. Ladle the seafood into the bread lower and top with sauce bowls.

Barbecued Grouper

Makes 4 servings

**Grill
temperature**

medium-high

Grouper is one of my favorite types of fish, but if you can't find it, the recipe works just as well with mako, tuna, marlin, or even shrimp. The barbecue sauce is basically a vinaigrette, and the flavor keeps improving every day in the refrigerator.

>**2 cups Grilling Vinaigrette (page 144)**
>
>**¼ cup catsup**
>
>**¼ cup honey**
>
>**¼ cup chopped scallion**
>
>**2 tablespoons chopped fresh ginger**
>
>**2 tablespoons soy sauce**
>
>**I teaspoon Worcestershire sauce**
>
>**2 pounds grouper fillets**
>
>**2 cucumbers, peeled, seeded, and sliced**

Combine the vinaigrette, catsup, honey, scallion, ginger, soy sauce, and Worcestershire sauce in a medium bowl and mix well. Place the fish in a heatproof baking dish and pour the sauce over it. Marinate for 10 to 15 minutes. Place the baking dish on the grill and cook for 2 minutes. Turn the fish and cook 6 to 7 minutes longer. (The sauce should be boiling when the fish is done.) To serve, arrange the cucumbers on a serving dish, place the fish on top, and spoon the sauce over the fish.

Charcoal-Grilled Trout

Makes 4 servings

Use hardwood such as oak for this dish, or flavor the heat source with soaked wood chips, such as mesquite or hickory. The simple flavor of the trout will be enhanced by the smoke.

Grill temperature

high

> **Four 1-pound brook trout, cleaned**
>
> **Juice of 2 lemons**
>
> **1 tablespoon chopped fresh parsley**
>
> **½ teaspoon Tabasco sauce**
>
> **Fresh lemon slices**

Start a charcoal or wood fire 45 to 60 minutes before grilling. Once the fire has been lit, marinate the trout in the lemon juice, parsley, and Tabasco in the refrigerator. When the fire is ready, place the trout on the grill (or use a fish basket) and cook for 4 to 5 minutes on each side, frequently basting the fish with the marinade. Garnish with lemon slices.

Swordfish
with Papaya Salsa

Makes 4 servings

Although this recipe calls for swordfish, you can use mako, tuna, or marlin. Just be sure you don't overcook the steaks. We serve swordfish at the restaurant with different kinds of salsa—black bean, roasted red pepper, or papaya—depending on our mood.

> ¼ **cup olive oil**
>
> ¼ **cup white wine**
>
> 2 **tablespoons cane syrup or dark corn syrup**
>
> **Juice and zest of 1 lime**
>
> **Ground black pepper to taste**
>
> ¼ **teaspoon Tabasco sauce**
>
> **Four 7- to 8-ounce swordfish steaks**
>
> **1 recipe Papaya Salsa (recipe follows)**

Combine the oil, wine, cane syrup, lime juice and zest, pepper, and Tabasco in a shallow bowl. Marinate the swordfish steaks in this mixture for 30 minutes in the refrigerator, turning the fish twice. Grill the steaks for 4 to 5 minutes on each side. Serve with cool Papaya Salsa.

182

Grilling
with
Chef
George
Hirsch

Papaya Salsa

I ripe papaya, skinned, seeded, and diced

4 plum tomatoes, seeded and diced

I cucumber, peeled, seeded, and diced

¼ cup chopped scallion

2 tablespoons chopped fresh mint

I tablespoon honey

Combine all of the ingredients in a medium bowl. Set aside for 1 hour, unrefrigerated.

Stir-fried Shrimp
with Garlic

Makes 4 servings

**Grill
temperature**

medium-high

A wok works very well on an outdoor grill, but if the handle on yours is plastic, it may melt if left over the heat source too long. Make sure all the ingredients are ready before you begin to cook; once you start stir-frying, you shouldn't stop. If hoisin sauce is not available, mix together equal parts of honey, catsup, and soy sauce.

1 ½ pounds large shrimp (16 to 20 per pound)

¼ cup vegetable oil

4 cloves garlic, chopped

1 tablespoon chopped fresh ginger

2 tablespoons chopped red bell pepper

¼ cup coconut milk

1 tablespoon hoisin sauce

1 tablespoon chopped fresh basil

3 cups chopped Napa (or other) cabbage

Peel and devein the shrimp. Heat a wok on the grill and add the oil. When the oil is hot, add the garlic and ginger, and stir-fry for 2 minutes. Add the shrimp and red pepper, and stir-fry for 2 minutes. Add the coconut milk, hoisin sauce, and basil, and continue stir-frying until the shrimp is opaque. Serve over the cabbage.

184

Grilling
with
Chef
George
Hirsch

Grilled
Shrimp Cocktail

Makes 4 servings

Rather than being boiled up on the stove, these shrimp are cooked on the barbecue. You could marinate them in the Southwest Marinade, but that would be gilding the lily.

6 bamboo skewers

1 pound large shrimp (16 to 20 per pound), unpeeled

¼ cup olive oil

1 recipe Dori's Cocktail Sauce (recipe follows)

Soak the skewers in water for 30 minutes. Thread the shrimp on the skewers and brush them with oil. Place the skewers on the grill and cook for 4 to 5 minutes, turning once. As soon as the shrimp are cooked, place the skewers in ice water until the shrimp are well chilled. Remove the shrimp from the skewers, peel, and chill until ready to serve. Serve with Dori's Cocktail Sauce.

Grill temperature

medium-high

Dori's Cocktail Sauce

Makes about 1 cup

Ever since my daughter Dori was three or four (she's ten now), she has wanted to be in the kitchen. She actually came up with this cocktail sauce, and it's pretty good. If you want to get your children involved in helping prepare dinner, here's a good recipe to start with.

½ **cup catsup**

¼ **cup chili sauce**

1 ½ **teaspoons horseradish**

¼ **teaspoon Tabasco sauce**

Black pepper to taste

½ **teaspoon soy sauce (optional)**

Combine all of the ingredients in a medium bowl, mix well and chill.

186

Grilling
with
Chef
George
Hirsch

Red Snapper with
Macadamia and Wheat Crust

Makes 4 servings

After some friends and I spent a warm March day on a 30-foot sailboat in Florida, we were all very hungry. We stopped at the market and picked up some fish, but when we got to my friend's house, we had to make do with what he had in the cupboard: half a box of Triscuits, a jar of macadamia nuts, and a bottle of Italian dressing. This is the result.

2 pounds red snapper fillets

2 cups Grilling Vinaigrette (page 144) or Italian dressing

6 ounces macadamia nuts

2 cups Triscuits or wheat crackers

Place the snapper fillets in a nonreactive dish and pour the vinaigrette over them. Marinate for 30 minutes in the refrigerator, turning the fish twice.

Chop or grind the nuts and crackers very fine in a food processor or blender.

Remove the snapper from the marinade. Place the fish on a lightly oiled grill for 30 seconds; turn and cook 30 seconds longer. Remove the fish and place it in an ovenproof baking dish. Pour the grilling vinaigrette over the fish and cover with the nut-crumb mixture. Continue grilling until the fish is done, about 8 to 12 minutes, depending on the thickness. (The fish will turn from opaque to light white in color when it's done.) Do not overcook.

Grilled
Warm Calamari Salad

Only a short time ago, calamari was considered an ethnic food and was sold exclusively in ethnic markets. Today, if you can't buy it frozen at your local supermarket, chances are your fish store will have it. This salad, flavored with lemongrass, lime juice, and mint leaves, has definite Thai leanings. Warm or chilled, it's delicious.

1 pound calamari, cleaned

1 onion, cut into ¼-inch slices

½ cup olive oil

¼ cup chopped scallion

5 cloves Caramelized Garlic (page 111)

3 to 4 red chile peppers, chopped (optional)

1 stalk lemongrass, chopped fine

10 to 12 fresh mint leaves, chopped

Juice and zest of 3 to 4 limes

¼ cup olive oil

Half 1-ounce package bean threads or 1 cup cooked vermicelli

1 large cucumber, peeled, seeded, and sliced

1 head frissee or curly endive, washed and dried

188

Grilling
with
Chef
George
Hirsch

Cut the calamari bodies into ¼-inch rings and leave the tentacles whole, or cut them into 2-inch pieces. Brush the calamari and onion slices with the ½ cup olive oil.

To make the dressing, combine the scallion, garlic, chile pepper, lemongrass, mint, lime juice and zest, and the ¼ cup olive oil in a small bowl and mix well. Soak the bean threads in hot water for 15 to 20 minutes, or until they soften. Drain and pat dry.

Arrange the cucumber and frissee on a serving platter. Arrange the bean threads on top.

Grill the onion slices for 4 to 5 minutes on each side. Grill the calamari until they turn opaque, about 2 minutes; do not overcook. Toss the cooked calamari with the dressing. Place the onion rings on the bean threads and top with the calamari. Serve at room temperature.

Oyster Pie

Oyster pie is similar to clam pie, but it doesn't have a double crust. Slices of stale bread brushed with oil become crispy on the grill and form the bottom crust. Be careful not to overcook the oysters.

Grill temperature

medium

I tablespoon butter

I cup diced onion

I cup diced celery

½ cup diced carrot

2 cloves garlic, chopped

2 tablespoons all-purpose flour

2 cups potatoes cut into ¼-inch dice

4 cups fish stock

2 cups milk

Pinch ground nutmeg

I bay leaf

¼ teaspoon Tabasco sauce

8 thin slices day-old bread, preferably French or Italian

2 dozen shucked medium oysters

½ cup seasoned bread crumbs

Heat the butter in a 4-quart saucepan on the grill. Add the onion, celery, carrot, and garlic, and sauté slowly for 5 to 6 minutes. Stir in the flour and cook for 4 to 5 minutes, stirring constantly. Add the potato and slowly whisk

190

Grilling
with
Chef
George
Hirsch

in the stock and milk. Add the nutmeg, bay leaf, and Tabasco; cook for 10 to 12 minutes, or until the potato is tender. Remove the bay leaf.

Line a 10-inch deep-dish pie pan with the bread and arrange the oysters on top. Spoon the vegetables over the oysters. Top with the bread crumbs and grill for 15 to 20 minutes.

Salmon with a Basil and Red Pepper Crust

Makes 4 servings

The flavor of basil blends well with the taste of salmon. Chopped red pepper, garlic, Parmesan cheese, and bread crumbs combine to make an unusual crumb topping on the baked fillets.

1 ½ red bell peppers, seeded and chopped fine

3 cloves garlic

½ cup fresh basil leaves

¼ cup olive oil

2 tablespoons grated Parmesan cheese

1 cup fresh bread crumbs

Four 7-ounce salmon fillets

Combine the pepper, garlic, and basil in the bowl of a food processor and process until pureed. With the motor going, drizzle in the oil and cheese. Stir in the bread crumbs. Spread the mixture evenly on the fish and place in a nonstick pan or black cast-iron skillet. Place the pan on the grill, cover, and cook for 10 to 12 minutes, or until the salmon is pink and the bread-crumb mixture is set.

192

Grilling
with
Chef
George
Hirsch

Farm-Raised Catfish Fillets with a Pecan-Corn Crust

Makes 4 servings

Farm-raised catfish have a milky-white flesh and a nice sweet taste. The addition of pecans to the cornmeal gives the crust a nice crunch.

Grill temperature

medium-high

2 cups Milk Marinade for Seafood (page 158)

2 pounds farm-raised catfish fillets

1 cup fine cornmeal or *masa harina*

½ cup all-purpose flour

¼ cup ground pecans

Vegetable oil

Lemon slices

1 recipe Rémoulade (page 159)

Place the marinade in a shallow bowl. Add the catfish and marinate for at least 1 hour in the refrigerator.

Combine the cornmeal, flour, and ground pecans in a shallow dish and dredge the catfish fillets in this mixture.

Grease a heavy black cast-iron skillet or a heavy-duty cookie sheet generously with vegetable oil, and preheat. Place the fillets in the skillet and grill for 4 to 5 minutes on each side, or until light brown. Serve with fresh lemon slices and Rémoulade.

Cane-Charred Shrimp

Makes 4 servings

Using rosemary sprigs as skewers lends a pungent flavor to these shrimp marinated in a sweet mixture of cane syrup and wine. The sugar caramelizes during grilling, making the shrimp very appealing, and the marinade gives them a real kick. Serve as a salad over greens or with pasta.

Cane-Charred Marinade

1 cup olive oil

¼ cup cane syrup or dark corn syrup

½ cup white wine

3 shallots, chopped fine

Juice of 1 lemon

¼ teaspoon Tabasco sauce

½ teaspoon dried rosemary

½ teaspoon dried thyme

1 pound large shrimp (16 to 20 per pound)

4 large sprigs rosemary, soaked in oil

1 bunch arugula, cleaned and trimmed

Lemon slices for garnish

194

Grilling
with
Chef
George
Hirsch

Combine the oil, cane syrup, wine, shallot, lemon juice, Tabasco, rosemary, and thyme in a shallow dish.

Thread the shrimp onto the rosemary sprigs and marinate for 15 to 20 minutes in the mixture. Remove the sprig skewers and place them on the grill until the shrimp are lightly charred, about 2 minutes. Move them to medium heat to finish cooking, about 4 to 8 minutes. Arrange the skewers on the arugula and garnish with the lemon slices.

Freshwater Bass
in a Pouch

When I was growing up, our family frequently went camping in Canada. My father was never a world-class chef, but he is a great gourmand and loves to eat good food. He would take us fishing, and I can still remember the flavor of the fish that came out of the lake and were literally thrown onto the fire. The outside got charred and the inside was sweet and moist.

It may be my imagination, but I find that this recipe works best if you have a lake, stream, river, or ocean within walking distance of a wood or charcoal fire. Perhaps it's because after fishing all day, the anticipation of waiting for the coals to get red-hot makes the fish taste that much better. Or perhaps the absolute freshness of the fish stands above any camouflage of seasonings or accompaniments.

Other freshwater fish, such as perch and pike, can be substituted for bass.

A day's catch of bass, either fresh- or saltwater

Margarine or vegetable oil

Salt and pepper to taste

196

Scale and gut the fish. Place each fish on a large piece of aluminum foil (enough to go around the fish twice), dot with margarine or brush with oil, and season with salt and pepper. Wrap the fish and place them on the fire. A 2-pound fish will take about 18 to 20 minutes.

Mahimahi with
Orange and Cilantro

Makes 4 servings

Mahimahi is very popular in Hawaii and the Pacific Northwest, and its reputation for being a tasty fish is slowly making its way toward the East Coast. This simple dish gets its sweetness from the orange and its pungency from the cilantro.

Grill temperature

medium

½ **cup fresh orange juice**

½ **cup olive oil**

½ **cup orange segments**

2 tablespoons chopped cilantro

3 scallions, chopped fine

¼ **cup white wine**

¼ **teaspoon Tabasco sauce**

¼ **teaspoon Worcestershire sauce**

Four 8-ounce mahimahi fillets

Combine the orange juice, olive oil, orange segments, cilantro, scallion, white wine, Tabasco, and Worcestershire sauce in a shallow bowl and mix well. Marinate the fish in this mixture for at least 1 hour in the refrigerator. Place the fish and the marinade in a nonstick skillet and grill for 4 to 5 minutes. Remove the fish and set it aside. Reduce the marinade and pour it over the fish.

Seafood Sausage

Makes 4 to 6 servings

Grill temperature

medium

This is probably the most difficult dish in this book because it has so many steps. Consider it a recipe for advanced grilloholics.

Ask your butcher to sell you some sausage casing. Tie a knot at the end of each casing, and fit it onto the end of a funnel with a ½-inch opening. Fill the funnel with the sausage mixture and push it through the funnel stem into the casing. Twist the sausage every 5 inches to make links, and prick the sausages with a fork before simmering them in milk.

1 tablespoon butter

1 cup finely diced onion

8 ounces squid, cleaned and chopped

8 ounces salmon

8 ounces crabmeat or peeled shrimp

1 pound sole fillets

2 eggs

1 cup heavy cream

¼ cup chopped black olives

1 tablespoon chopped cilantro

¼ teaspoon Tabasco sauce

¼ teaspoon Worcestershire sauce

Sausage casing

4 cups milk

Spicy mustard

198

Grilling
with
Chef
George
Hirsch

In a large nonstick skillet on the grill or stovetop, heat the butter and cook the onion over low heat. Do not allow the onion to brown.

Poach the squid, salmon, and crabmeat in water to cover until tender. Cut the sole into small pieces, combine with the onion and cooked seafood, and puree in a food processor. Place the mixture in a bowl and add the eggs, cream, olives, cilantro, Tabasco, and Worcestershire sauce. Mix well and pack into the casings.

Heat the milk in a nonstick skillet on the grill or stovetop and, when it begins to simmer, add the sausage. When the milk returns to a simmer, cook the sausage for 15 minutes. Remove the sausage and allow to cool. Place the sausage on the grill and cook, turning once, until hot, about 3 to 5 minutes. Serve with spicy mustard.

Fresh Tuna Burger

Makes 4 servings

Grill
temperature

high

When you think burger these days, you don't have to think beef or turkey. Meaty tuna, marinated in a flavorful Pacific Rim marinade, makes a nice switch. Be sure to keep the tuna cold during preparation.

1 ½ pounds fresh tuna, either yellowfin, blue, or albacore

2 egg whites, lightly beaten

1 teaspoon chopped cilantro

¼ teaspoon lime zest

¼ teaspoon Tabasco sauce

1 teaspoon Dijon mustard

1 recipe Pacific Rim Marinade (page 148)

4 burger buns

1 bunch arugula

Cut the tuna into 1-inch pieces and place them in the bowl of a food processor. Using an on-off motion, grind the tuna for 45 to 60 seconds, or until it is chopped but not pureed. (Overprocessing the tuna will make it warm.)

Transfer the tuna to a bowl, stir in the egg whites, and mix well. Add the cilantro, lime zest, Tabasco, and mustard, and blend well. Shape the tuna mixture into four burgers. Place them in the marinade and refrigerate 2 to 3 hours.

Place the burgers on the grill and cook them for 3 to 4 minutes on each side, or until rare or medium-rare. (Cooking the burgers longer will dry them out.) Place each burger on a burger bun and serve on a bed of arugula.

200

Grilling
with
Chef
George
Hirsch

Game

Game is generally considered to be meat from the furred or feathered living in the wild and nothing is more American than home on the range.

Unless you bag it yourself, or know a friendly hunter, all the game found in today's marketplace has been farm-raised in this country or abroad and is U.S. Department of Agriculture–inspected.

And because the game has been fed a controlled diet, the flesh has a less gamy flavor. But game is expensive, so don't waste it on finicky eaters.

Venison Chili

Grill
temperature

high,
then low;
indirect
cooking

There are hundreds of chili recipes, and each one is a little different. This basic chili recipe combines several flavors of the Southwest. Turkey or beef can be substituted for the venison. Or make it vegetarian, using eggplant, squash, and onion in place of the meat.

2 tablespoons olive oil

3 strips bacon, chopped fine

1 cup diced onion

6 cloves garlic, chopped

1 ½ pounds venison, cut into ¼-inch dice

2 cups chopped tomatoes, fresh or canned

12 ounces amber or dark beer

½ cup chopped scallion

2 tablespoons crushed dried peppers, such as ancho or serrano

3 fresh jalapeño peppers, seeded and chopped

1 tablespoon dried cumin

1 tablespoon dried coriander

1 tablespoon dried oregano

1 tablespoon dried basil

1 tablespoon cider vinegar

1 teaspoon Worcestershire sauce

½ teaspoon Tabasco sauce

½ teaspoon ground cinnamon

Salt and pepper to taste

One 16-ounce can black beans, rinsed and drained

1 recipe Grilled Polenta (page 91)

In a large stockpot over high heat on the grill or stovetop, heat the oil. Add the bacon, onion, and garlic, and sauté for 5 minutes, stirring occasionally. Add the venison and cook, stirring frequently, until the meat is lightly browned. Add the tomato, beer, scallion, dried pepper, jalapeño pepper, cumin, coriander, oregano, basil, vinegar, Worcestershire sauce, Tabasco, cinnamon, salt, and pepper. Stir well and cook over low heat for about 1½ hours, stirring occasionally. Stir in the black beans and cook 15 minutes longer, or until the venison is tender. Serve over Grilled Polenta.

Pheasant with Ricotta-and-Herb Stuffing

Makes 4 servings

Most of us think of putting the stuffing inside the bird. In this recipe, however, it's placed between the skin and the flesh, where it imparts flavor to the meat, while keeping the breast moist and preventing it from overcooking.

I cup ricotta

¼ pound bacon

¼ cup chopped onion

6 medium mushrooms

Juice of I orange

2 tablespoons butter, softened

I tablespoon chopped scallion

I teaspoon dried thyme

I teaspoon dried rosemary

Salt and pepper to taste

2 pheasants, about I¼ to I½ pounds each

2 tablespoons olive oil

Place the ricotta in a strainer, and with the back of a tablespoon, press out and discard any liquid.

In the bowl of a food processor, combine the bacon, onion, mushrooms, orange juice, butter, scallion, thyme, rosemary, salt, and pepper, and process until smooth. Add the drained ricotta and process 30 seconds longer.

Lift the flap of neck skin of each pheasant, slip your hand in, and carefully separate the skin from the flesh, taking care not to break the skin. Using half the ricotta mixture for each bird, fill the space over the breast and thigh with the stuffing. Once the stuffing is in place, flatten out the skin with your hand so that the stuffing is evenly distributed and lies flat.

Insert the rotisserie rod through the pheasants, making sure they're balanced and secure with holding forks. Brush the pheasants with the olive oil and insert the rod in the rotisserie mechanism. Grill on medium heat for 10 minutes and stop the rotisserie. Wrap the pheasants in aluminum foil and grill them for 20 minutes on medium-low, removing the foil for the last 5 minutes. The pheasants are done when the juices in the thigh run clear when pierced with a fork or when the meat registers 180°F. on an instant-read thermometer.

Maple-Roasted Quail Salad with Hazelnut Dressing

Makes 4 servings

Grill temperature

medium

I've combined quail and hazelnuts, two regional foods of the Northwest, to make a sweet, crispy, poultry salad. Boneless quail are sold at most butcher shops, but if your butcher doesn't have them on hand, they can be ordered. To toast hazelnuts, place them in a pan on the grill for 5 to 7 minutes, shaking the pan occasionally so they don't burn.

¼ **cup maple syrup**

2 **cups apple juice**

I **tablespoon chopped fresh rosemary**

Juice of I lemon

4 **boneless quail, 4 to 5 ounces each**

6 **to 8 cups bitter greens, such as frissee or Belgian endive**

I **recipe Hazelnut Dressing (page 143)**

Combine the maple syrup, apple juice, rosemary, and lemon juice in a bowl. Marinate the quail in this mixture for 1 to 2 hours in the refrigerator.

Remove the quail from the marinade and grill for 3 to 4 minutes on each side. Toss the bitter greens with the Hazelnut Dressing and arrange the quail on top.

206

Grilling
with
Chef
George
Hirsch

Lamb

Alben Barkley, vice president and U.S. senator, once proclaimed that in Kentucky a politician's skill in getting votes was in direct proportion to his ability to speak eloquently at picnics and barbecues, especially, where the meat of choice was a rare and juicy piece of lamb roasting over an open spit.

Lamb takes extremely well to grilling because it's well marbled and highly flavored. The herbs of choice are rosemary and thyme and Americans have learned that they can never use too much garlic when they cook lamb.

Lamb *Osso Buco* Style

Makes 4 servings

Osso buco usually calls for veal shanks, but lamb shanks adapt very well to the recipe. They don't take quite as long to cook as veal shanks, are more readily available, and they have the same sweet flavor. *Osso buco*, which literally means "bone with a hole," can be served over polenta or risotto.

Grill temperature

medium-high, then low, then high

¼ **cup all-purpose flour**

Salt and pepper to taste

Four 10-ounce lamb shanks, trimmed

2 tablespoons olive oil

I onion, chopped

3 cloves garlic, chopped

2 ribs celery, diced

2 carrots, diced

I cup drained canned plum tomatoes

I cup dry red wine

I teaspoon dried rosemary

I teaspoon dried thyme

3 bay leaves

2 cups chicken stock

208

Grilling

with

Chef

George

Hirsch

Place a large cast-iron skillet on a medium-high grill. Season the flour with the salt and pepper and dredge the shanks in this mixture, shaking off any excess. Heat the oil in the skillet and sear the shanks on all sides until they are light brown. Remove them and set aside. Add the onion and garlic to the pan and cook until the onion browns slightly.

Add the celery and carrot and cook for 2 to 3 minutes. Return the shanks to the skillet along with the tomato, wine, rosemary, thyme, bay leaves, and stock. Cover and simmer on low heat for 1½ hours, or until the meat is tender. Remove the shanks, set them aside, and keep them warm. Discard the bay leaves.

Remove any fat from top of the sauce. Place the skillet on the grill over high heat, bring to a boil, and cook for 5 minutes to reduce the sauce and thicken it.

Smoked Shoulder of Lamb

Makes 10 to 12 servings

Indirect
cooking

Lamb is a natural for smoking because of its high fat content. Some excess fat can be cut off, but there are lines of fat that run through the meat that baste the lamb as it smokes and keep it moist and tender. The cola in the water pan gives the lamb a tangy sweet flavor.

**One 7- to 8-pound lamb shoulder, boned and trimmed of sinew
   (leave fat on)**

1 cup red wine

½ cup sugar

6 cloves garlic

2 teaspoons dried rosemary

2 teaspoons dried thyme

2 teaspoons dried parsley

½ teaspoon Tabasco sauce

½ teaspoon Worcestershire sauce

Salt and pepper to taste

One 2-liter bottle cola

Prepare smoker.

Combine the wine, sugar, garlic, rosemary, thyme, parsley, Tabasco, Worcestershire, salt, and pepper in a bowl large enough to accommodate the lamb shoulder. Marinate the meat overnight in the refrigerator.

Presoak pecan chips or grapevine cuttings in cold water for 1 hour. Drain off the water and place the wood in the smoker. Remove the lamb from the marinade. Heat the smoker. Place the cola and marinade in the water pan and put the lamb on the top rack. Smoke for 5 hours and check the internal temperature with an instant-read thermometer for desired doneness. It should read 120°F.

Leg of Lamb in the Style of
Cochon à la Broche

Makes 10 to 12 servings

Leg of lamb in the style of *cochon à la broche*, or spit-roasted pig, employs a slow, dry-cooking method (in contrast to lamb cooked *cochon de lait* style (page 213), which is marinated and roasted by a slow, moist method.

Serve the lamb medium or medium-rare. To avoid flare-ups from the fat, place a water pan directly below the lamb to catch drippings.

> **One 12-pound leg whole of lamb, trimmed of all but ¼ inch of**
> **surface fat**
> **1 tablespoon paprika**
> **½ tablespoon cayenne**
> **½ tablespoon black pepper**
> **6 cloves garlic, chopped fine**
> **½ teaspoon ground nutmeg**
> **1 tablespoon dried basil**
> **3 bay leaves, crushed**
> **1 cup dry red wine**

212

**Grilling
with
Chef
George
Hirsch**

Split and bone the leg of lamb, but leave the shank bone attached. (Or have your butcher do it.) Combine the paprika, cayenne, black pepper, garlic, nutmeg, basil, and bay leaves in a small bowl and mix well. Season the meat, inside and out, with the mixture. Tie the roast with butcher's twine, secure it on the rotisserie spit, and begin cooking.

Place a small pan of water directly under the roast to catch dripping fat and reduce flare-ups. Baste the meat frequently with the lamb drippings and the red wine. Cook for 15 to 20 minutes per pound, or until it reaches the desired doneness. (An instant-read thermometer should register 120°F. for medium-rare.)

Leg of Lamb
in the Style of
Cochon de Lait

Makes 8 to 10 servings

Cochon de lait is an Acadian food celebration that centers around marinating and slow-roasting a 35-pound suckling pig for several hours. Of course, while the pig is cooking, the Acadians are celebrating food and the quality of life. They dance and talk about food, and then they eat the food and talk about more food.

At the restaurant we had a request for a Kosher menu, so we adapted the marinating flavors and roasting concept behind *cochon de lait* and substituted a leg of lamb for the pig. We liked it so much we've served it that way ever since.

(continued)

Grill temperature

build a hot hardwood fire or charcoal fire 45 minutes before cooking lamb; indirect cooking

Lamb

½ cup cane syrup or dark corn syrup

2 tablespoons Tabasco sauce

6 cloves garlic, chopped

Juice of 1 lemon

1 tablespoon crushed dried rosemary

1 tablespoon dried thyme

½ tablespoon freshly ground black pepper

One 4- to 5-pound leg of lamb, split or trussed

Combine the cane syrup, Tabasco, garlic, lemon juice, rosemary, thyme, and pepper in a small bowl and mix well. Rub the mixture onto all sides of the lamb. Marinate for 1 hour at room temperature or for 3 to 4 hours in the refrigerator.

Place the lamb on the grill for 35 to 40 minutes, letting the outside brown well. Transfer the lamb to a disposable foil pan, cover, and place it back on the fire for 15 minutes. Lamb should be medium done.

Remove the lamb from the heat and let it rest for 30 minutes before slicing.

Pork

There's an old adage in European cultures that every part of the pig can be used expect the oink. This couldn't be more on the mark. The more tender cuts, such as the loins and the hams, lend themselves to grilling, the shoulders can be smoked, and whatever is left over can usually be ground up and made into sausages.

Grilled Ham Steak with Mustard–Ginger Ale Sauce

Makes 4 servings

Grilled ham steak is the perfect choice for a very simple and quick meal. The ham steak is rinsed first to wash off any excess salt. Adding ginger ale to the sauce gives it an elusive tang. Ham steak is a natural with sweet potato home-fries.

One 2-pound ham steak, cut ½ to ¾ inch thick

12 ounces ginger ale

2 tablespoons honey

¼ cup Dijon mustard

1 tablespoon chopped fresh mint

¼ teaspoon Tabasco sauce

Pinch ground coriander

Rinse the ham steak in cold water. In a medium bowl, combine the remaining ingredients and mix well. Grill the ham steak on one side and turn it after 4 to 5 minutes (it will turn light brown). Baste with half the sauce. Move the ham to a cooler edge of the grill and cook for 10 to 12 minutes, basting occasionally. Serve the remaining sauce on the side.

216

Grilling
with
Chef
George
Hirsch

Barbecued
Pork Tenderloin

Makes 6 servings

This dish is simple to make and fairly economical because the pork is boneless and has very little fat. Just remember to dry-rub the meat in the morning. Cut up any leftovers and make sandwiches or add to a tossed salad.

Grill
temperature

medium

> ½ cup Pork Dry Rub (page 156)
>
> Two 1¼-pound pork tenderloins
>
> 1 cup Honey Pork Sauce (page 151)

Cut off any excess fat from the pork and remove any sinew. Cover the pork on all sides with the dry rub and refrigerate for 8 hours. Grill the pork for 10 to 12 minutes, turning occasionally. Baste with Honey Pork Sauce during the last 5 minutes.

Braised Stuffed Pork Chops

Makes 4 servings

Prepare this recipe when you want to impress some guests or your in-laws. Make the stuffing ahead of time and chill it. Then all you have to do at the last minute is cook the chops on top of the grill, and you'll get rave reviews. You can buy double-cut pork chops at the butcher with pockets already in them.

4 double-cut, center loin pork chops, approximately 1 inch thick

1 cup finely diced, day-old French or Italian bread

½ cup heavy cream

2 tablespoons butter

2 to 3 shallots, chopped fine

1 cup sliced shiitake mushrooms

¼ cup finely chopped prosciutto or smoked ham

¼ cup Madeira or sherry

Salt and pepper to taste

¼ cup all-purpose flour

Pinch ground nutmeg

Pinch cayenne

2 tablespoons olive oil

½ cup chopped onion

½ cup dry red wine

2 cups chicken stock

2 bay leaves

218

Grilling
with
Chef
George
Hirsch

Cut a 1-inch slit along the back side of each chop. Insert the knife and enlarge the slit inside the meat, leaving a ½-inch space around the inside perimeter uncut.

In a small bowl, combine the bread and cream and let sit until the bread is softened.

On the grill or stovetop, heat the butter in a skillet and sauté the shallot for 2 minutes. Add the mushrooms, prosciutto, and Madeira, and cook for 2 minutes. Remove the pan from the heat and add the softened bread, and salt and pepper to taste. Mix well and chill the mixture in the refrigerator.

Place a quarter of the stuffing in each pork-chop pocket and secure the edges with toothpicks. Combine the flour with black pepper to taste, nutmeg, and cayenne. Dredge the chops in the seasoned flour.

Place a black cast-iron skillet on the grill and heat the oil. Add the chops and sear them on both sides, about 3 to 4 minutes. Add the onion and cook for 2 to 3 minutes. Add the wine, stock, bay leaves, and salt and pepper to taste. Cover tightly and cook for 35 minutes over low heat. Discard the bay leaves. Remove the toothpicks from the chops before serving.

Country
Fried Pork Chops

Makes 6 servings

Grill temperature

medium-high

These pork chops are covered with a crumb mixture and cooked in a heavy skillet right on top of the grill. Serve them with mashed potatoes and bitter greens.

6 loin pork chops, cut ½ inch thick

½ cup all-purpose flour

2 eggs, beaten

2 cups seasoned bread crumbs

Vegetable oil

Dredge the pork chops in flour and dip them in the beaten eggs. Press the bread crumbs onto both sides of the chops. Grease a heavy-duty pan with vegetable oil and lay the chops on top. Brush the tops of the chops generously with oil. Place the pan on the grill and cook until golden brown, about 8 to 10 minutes on each side.

220

Grilling

with

Chef

George

Hirsch

Grilled Pork Spareribs

Makes 4 servings

Everyone has a different style of cooking spareribs; one popular way is to boil the ribs before grilling them. I like to season the ribs, place them in a roasting pan, add water, cover, and pan cook. This method does help tenderize the ribs and removes excess fat so there is less chance of flare-ups over the fire, but it's a trade-off: There is a very definite loss of flavor.

Grill
temperature

medium,
then low

> **4 pounds spareribs**
>
> **1 recipe Pork Dry Rub (page 156)**
>
> **4 quarts boiling water**
>
> **3 bay leaves**
>
> **1 teaspoon Tabasco sauce**
>
> **1 tablespoon Worcestershire sauce**
>
> **1 recipe Sweet Pork Sauce (page 151)**

Trim any excess fat from the ribs and peel off the skin. Cover the ribs on all sides with pork rub, place in a roasting pan, and refrigerate for 24 hours.

Combine the boiling water, bay leaves, Tabasco, and Worcestershire sauce; pour over the ribs. Place the ribs on a medium grill and cook for 10 minutes. Remove the ribs and discard the cooking liquid. Place the ribs over low heat for 35 to 40 minutes, turning occasionally. Baste the ribs during the last 10 minutes with the pork sauce.

Pork Medallion Salad

Grill
temperature

medium

You'll love the contrast of the warm pork medallions hot off the grill with the crisp cabbage, cool cucumber, crunchy noodles, and soft fruit. The dressing is simply pineapple juice and mint. Don't cut the pork medallions too thin or they'll cook too quickly.

I pound pork tenderloin

2 tablespoons hoisin sauce

¼ cup white wine or rice wine

I tablespoon chopped fresh ginger

I teaspoon sesame oil

I teaspoon hot chili oil (optional)

½ teaspoon ground star anise, or I ounce sambucca

2 teaspoons peanut oil

2 cups shredded Napa or Savoy cabbage

½ cucumber, peeled, sliced, and seeded

½ red bell pepper, cut into small slices

4 scallions, cut on the bias into I-inch pieces

½ cup pineapple juice

2 tablespoons peanut oil

I tablespoon chopped fresh mint

222

Grilling
with
Chef
George
Hirsch

1 tablespoon toasted sesame seeds

4 large cabbage leaves

4 fresh figs

2 cups fried rice noodles (optional)

Trim the pork tenderloin and cut it into eight equal pieces. Pound each piece lightly until it's about ⅓ inch thick.

In a medium nonreactive bowl, combine the hoisin sauce, wine, ginger, sesame oil, hot chili oil, star anise, and peanut oil. Add the pork and marinate for 1 to 2 hours in the refrigerator. Grill the medallions for 3 to 4 minutes on each side.

Place the cabbage, cucumber, red pepper, and scallion in a medium bowl and toss well.

Combine the pineapple juice, peanut oil, and mint, and whisk until well combined. Stir in the sesame seeds. Toss with the cabbage mixture.

Place a cabbage leaf on each of four plates. Arrange a quarter of the vegetable mixture on each leaf. Top each with two pieces of pork, and garnish with the fresh figs and fried rice noodles.

Sausage and Kraut

Makes 8 servings

Here's a recipe that combines four different types of sausage, sauerkraut, potatoes, and cannellini beans in a sweet-and-sour sauce. This is a good dish to make when you're feeding a crowd. Have some good-quality Dijon mustard and horseradish on hand, and don't forget some chewy brown bread and ice-cold beer.

½ **pound Italian-style sausage (hot or sweet)**

½ **pound weisswurst (white veal sausage)**

½ **pound knockwurst**

½ **pound smoked sausage, such as kielbasa**

2 **cups sauerkraut, rinsed**

10 to 12 **small new red potatoes**

1 **small onion, chopped**

4 **cloves garlic, chopped**

1 **cup white beans, soaked for 8 hours, or 2 cups canned cannellini
beans, added during the last 5 minutes of cooking**

¼ **cup cider vinegar**

2 **tablespoons sugar**

3 **bay leaves**

1 **tablespoon dried parsley**

Salt and pepper to taste

224

Grilling
with
Chef
George
Hirsch

Poke a few holes in all of the sausages with a fork so that the casings don't split. Cook the Italian sausage and the weisswurst about 30 minutes over medium heat on the grill, the knockwurst and the smoked sausage 10 minutes, turning several times.

Place the sausage in a large stockpot on the grill or stovetop. Add the remaining ingredients and cook for 1 hour over low to medium heat. Discard the bay leaves.

Roast Loin of Pork
on the Rotisserie

Makes 6 to 8 servings

Loin of pork is an excellent meat for the rotisserie. Grilling the roast indirectly means that there is less chance of a flare-up.

One 3- to 4-pound boneless pork loin

4 cloves garlic, chopped fine

I tablespoon crushed dried rosemary

I teaspoon dried parsley

I recipe Pork Baste (page 157)

Tie the pork loin at 1-inch intervals with butcher's twine or have the butcher do it. Rub the pork on all sides with the garlic, rosemary, and parsley. Thread the meat onto the rotisserie rod, set it in place, and put a drip pan beneath the meat. Cook for approximately 40 minutes per pound. After the first hour, brush the pork every 10 to 15 minutes with the pork baste.

Grill temperature

high; indirect cooking

225

Pork

Kielbasa
with Jelly Sauce

Makes 4 servings

Grill temperature

medium-low

When our friends John and Julie came over for a backyard barbecue and brought this dish along, I had them repeat the sauce ingredients several times because I couldn't believe what they were telling me. Were they serious? They were. Try this with crusty sourdough bread and a side of barbecue beans.

> 2 ½ **pounds kielbasa**
>
> I **cup grape jelly**
>
> I **cup catsup**
>
> I **tablespoon grated horseradish**
>
> I **teaspoon Tabasco sauce**
>
> I **teaspoon Worcestershire sauce**
>
> **Salt and pepper to taste**

Slice the kielbasa ¼ inch thick and place in a nonstick skillet. In a medium bowl, combine the remaining ingredients. Pour the sauce over the kielbasa, place the pan on the grill, and cook for 30 to 45 minutes.

226

Grilling
with
Chef
George
Hirsch

Poultry

If it seems that we eat a lot of poultry these days, it's probably because it's so economical and at the same time extremely versatile. Poultry is found in every course but dessert—appetizers, soups, salads, and entrees—and lends itself to every cooking method, from grilling to frying, roasting, and smoking. What's more, poultry is adaptable to just about any kind of added flavor, be it lemon, tomato, honey, soy sauce, mustard, or Tabasco. So whether you sauce it, stuff it, spit-roast it, or smoke it, you can't lose.

Lemon-and-Pepper Chicken

Makes 4 servings

If you're watching your fat and cholesterol intake, this dish can be made with boneless chicken breasts or chicken cutlets, which will cook in about half the time. When cooking chicken without the skin, be cautious not to overcook it. And because you don't want it to dry out, it should be basted more frequently. This American spin-off of a Thai dish should be drizzled with olive oil and served with fresh arugula and ripe summer fruit.

Juice of 3 lemons

2 teaspoons coarsely ground black pepper

½ cup olive oil

¼ cup dry white wine

I teaspoon dried thyme

I tablespoon chopped fresh parsley

½ teaspoon Tabasco sauce

¼ teaspoon Worcestershire sauce

One 3-pound chicken, cut into 8 pieces

Combine all of the ingredients except the chicken in a large shallow bowl. Add the chicken pieces and marinate for 1 hour in the refrigerator, turning occasionally.

Place the chicken on the grill and cook for 40 to 45 minutes, turning every 8 to 10 minutes and basting frequently with the marinade.

228

Grilling
with
Chef
George
Hirsch

Dijon Chicken Burger

Makes 4 to 6 servings

All white meat in a chicken burger might be a little too dry for most folks. The combination of light and dark meat makes it more flavorful and moist. Keeping the meat cold while mixing and storing it helps the burgers keep their shape and prevents the meat from spoiling.

Serve the burgers on rye or pumpernickel rolls with melted chèvre. Or leave off the cheese for a low-cholesterol, low-fat lunch.

**1½ pounds ground chicken (or grind ¾ pound chicken cutlet and
¾ pound boneless thigh meat)**

2 tablespoons Dijon mustard

1 teaspoon caraway seeds

1 tablespoon chopped scallion

Salt and pepper to taste

Olive oil

In a medium bowl, combine the chicken, mustard, caraway seeds, scallion, salt, and pepper and mix well. Shape into four to six burgers and refrigerate until well chilled, about 1 hour. Brush the burgers with olive oil, place them on the grill, and cook until no longer pink in the center, about 8 to 10 minutes, turning once.

Spit-Roasted Turkey

Makes 12 servings

After the turkey has been seasoned, I like to wrap it in foil and let it steam during the first 3 hours. When the foil is removed, I use the flavorful juices that collect to baste the bird until the skin becomes brown and crispy. To prevent flare-ups, place an aluminum pan under the turkey to collect drippings.

This cooking technique can be used with pheasant and chicken, but you have to be careful with duck because it's so fatty.

One 14- to 16-pound turkey

¼ cup olive oil

6 to 8 cloves garlic, coarsely chopped

4 to 5 whole sprigs rosemary

Freshly ground black pepper

6 strips salt pork or bacon

Rub the turkey with olive oil and place it on a large sheet of aluminum foil. Place the garlic, rosemary, pepper, and salt pork in the cavity of the turkey and wrap it securely in the foil. Lay the turkey upside-down on a second sheet of aluminum foil and secure the foil around the turkey. Thread the turkey on the rotisserie spit, following the manufacturer's directions, and cook for 3 hours.

Remove the turkey from the spit and place it in a pan; discard the foil and collect the juices. Continue cooking the turkey on the rotisserie 30 to 45

230

Grilling

with

Chef

George

Hirsch

minutes longer, basting frequently with the juices, until the skin is crispy and a meat thermometer inserted in the thigh reads 175°F.

Spit-Roasted Cornish Hens

Makes 4 servings

When my grandmother would spit-roast Cornish hens, she would baste them over and over again. I think this method is easier on the cook and results in a moist and juicy bird.

Four 1½-pound Cornish hens

2 oranges, sliced

8 sprigs fresh thyme

¼ cup honey

4 cloves garlic, chopped

Salt and pepper to taste

Place each hen on a 12-inch square of heavy-duty aluminum foil. Top the hens evenly with orange slices, thyme, honey, garlic, salt, and pepper. Wrap tightly, folding the edges over twice. Wrap again in foil. Secure on the rotisserie following the manufacturer's instructions. Cook the hens for 1 hour and remove them from the spit. Unwrap and discard the foil; reserve the juices. Return the hens to the spit and place a pan beneath them to catch the drippings. Continue cooking the hens for 30 minutes, basting frequently with the reserved juices.

Grill
temperature

medium;
indirect
cooking

Chicken 'n' Chive Dumplings

Makes 6 to 8 servings

This is a great dish for a camping or fishing trip, especially if you have a large black iron gumbo pot. Sit the pot over hot coals and build the fire around it. Once the cover is off, the stew will pick up a smoky flavor from the fire. Use self-rising flour or biscuit mix for the dumplings, and stand aside for those with hearty appetites.

One 4½- to 5-pound roaster hen, cut into pieces

2 cups chicken stock or water

I large onion, chopped

2 carrots, chopped

2 ribs celery, chopped

I parsnip, chopped (optional)

3 cloves garlic, chopped

2 bay leaves

2 tablespoons chopped fresh parsley

¼ teaspoon Tabasco sauce

Pepper and salt to taste

Dumplings

2 cups self-rising flour or biscuit mix

I ½ tablespoons shortening

2 tablespoons chopped fresh or freeze-dried chives

I cup milk

232

Grilling
with
Chef
George
Hirsch

In a large pot, preferably black cast iron, combine the chicken, chicken stock, onion, carrot, celery, parsnip, garlic, bay leaves, parsley, Tabasco, and pepper. Bring to a boil over high heat. Move the pot to a lower temperature and simmer for 1½ hours. Remove the chicken and continue to simmer the stew for 30 minutes. Remove the chicken meat from the bones and return it to the stew. Discard the bay leaves and season with salt.

To make the dumplings, mix the flour with the shortening and chives until well blended. Slowly add the milk, stirring constantly, until the mixture forms a dough. Drop the dough by heaping tablespoonful into the simmering broth and cook for 10 minutes. Cover and cook 10 minutes longer.

Brunswick Stew

Makes 4 servings

Hearty stews are usually cooked in a pot, but this is an exception. The ingredients are cooked in pouches, one to a person, which makes it a handy dish to take along on a camping trip. The pregrilled chicken and corn give the dish a nice smoky flavor.

One 2- to 3-pound chicken, cut into 8 pieces

¼ teaspoon dried thyme

¼ teaspoon dried rosemary

¼ teaspoon dried parsley

¼ teaspoon ground nutmeg

Four 14-inch sheets heavy-duty aluminum foil

4 strips bacon, chopped

2 large onions, chopped

16 small new potatoes, sliced

Kernels from 8 ears Montauk Indian Corn on the Cob (page 112), or
    one 12-ounce can corn niblets, drained

16 plum tomatoes, quartered

One 16-ounce can cannellini beans, drained

1 teaspoon Tabasco sauce

2 teaspoons Worcestershire sauce

Salt and pepper to taste

234

Grilling
with
Chef
George
Hirsch

Season the chicken with thyme, rosemary, parsley, and nutmeg, and grill on high heat for 8 to 10 minutes, or until brown, turning once.

Place the four sheets of foil on a flat surface. Place equal amounts of chicken on each piece of foil and top with equal amounts of bacon, onion, potato, corn, tomato, cannellini beans, Tabasco, Worcestershire sauce, salt, and pepper. Wrap each pouch, folding the edges over twice. Wrap once again in foil. Place the pouches on the grill for 50 minutes over medium heat, turning every 10 to 12 minutes.

Chicken with
Teriyaki Marinade

Makes 3 to 4 servings

Although this recipe calls for a whole cut-up chicken, you can use chicken breasts, but leave them in the marinade for no more than 30 minutes. The finished dish has a definite Asian flavor, so serve it with some hot cooked rice and stir-fried broccoli.

One 3-pound chicken, cut into 8 pieces

1 recipe Teriyaki Marinade (page 150)

Place the marinade in a nonreactive bowl. Add the chicken pieces and marinate for 45 minutes in the refrigerator. Remove the chicken and grill for 45 to 50 minutes, turning several times and basting frequently with the marinade.

Chicken Diablo

This version of "devil's chicken" is not the traditional tomato-based one; rather, it gets its red color from paprika. Skinless chicken parts can be used because the mustard-and-crumb mixture will keep the meat from drying out.

½ loaf white bread

Salt and pepper to taste

1 cup mustard

1 teaspoon paprika

1 teaspoon dried parsley

3 cloves garlic, chopped

1 teaspoon Tabasco sauce

One 2½- to 3-pound chicken, cut into 8 pieces

¾ cup vegetable oil

Process the bread in a food processor until it forms bread crumbs. Season the crumbs with salt and pepper. In a shallow dish, combine the mustard, paprika, parsley, garlic, and Tabasco. Roll the chicken in the mustard mixture and dredge it in bread crumbs.

Grease a heavy roasting pan with half the vegetable oil. Add the chicken pieces and drizzle them with the remaining oil. Place the pan on the grill over medium heat and cook for 25 minutes, turning the chicken every 8 to 10 minutes. Move the chicken to low temperature and cook for 20 to 25 minutes.

236

Grilling
with
Chef
George
Hirsch

Turkey Burger

When you make a burger, it's important to have the right proportion of lean to fat, both for flavor and tenderness. The average hamburger, for example, is 80 percent lean beef and 20 percent fat. The margarine, onion, and celery help keep this turkey burger moist. Avoid overcooking the burger or it will be dry and grainy.

Serve the burger with Fresh Cranberry Relish (page 240) on a soft roll or bun. Or, throw caution to the wind and wrap a slice or two of bacon around the burger before grilling.

2 tablespoons margarine

¼ cup finely minced onion

¼ cup finely minced celery

I teaspoon chopped fresh sage, or ¼ teaspoon dried sage

¼ cup very finely chopped pecans

I ½ pounds ground turkey, turkey tenderloin, or turkey cutlets

Olive oil

Heat the margarine in a small skillet. Sauté the onion and celery over medium-high heat on the grill or stovetop until the onion is transparent. Cool slightly and add the sage and pecans. Combine the onion mixture with the ground turkey and mix well. Shape into four to six burgers and chill well. Brush the burgers lightly with olive oil and grill over medium-low heat for 8 to 10 minutes, turning once.

Grilled Turkey Tenderloins with *Cacciatore* of White Beans and Escarole

Makes 4 servings

Cacciatore means "in the style of the hunter" and refers to cooking done out of doors using ingredients found in the countryside.

Grill temperature

medium, then low for sauce; high for turkey

1 pound fresh turkey tenderloins

5 tablespoons olive oil

Juice of ½ lemon

10 cloves garlic (2 minced, 8 left whole)

½ teaspoon dried basil

½ teaspoon dried oregano

¼ teaspoon freshly ground pepper

1 green bell pepper, seeded and diced

2 cups cooked cannellini beans, or one 19-ounce can cannellini beans, drained and rinsed under cold water

1 head escarole, rinsed and chopped

1 cup turkey or chicken broth

½ cup dry white wine

1 cup seeded and chopped plum tomatoes

3 sprigs fresh basil, chopped

¼ teaspoon freshly ground pepper

Chopped fresh Italian parsley

With a sharp knife, cut the turkey tenderloins on the diagonal into ¼-inch slices or medallions. In a shallow bowl, combine 2 tablespoons of the olive oil, the lemon juice, minced garlic, basil, oregano, and ground pepper, and mix well. Add the turkey and cover with the marinade. Cover the dish and refrigerate for 1 hour

Meanwhile, in a large skillet, heat the remaining 3 tablespoons of oil over medium heat on the grill or stovetop. Add the 8 whole garlic cloves and bell pepper, and sauté until the garlic is slightly golden, 3 to 5 minutes. Add the beans, escarole, broth, and wine. Stir slightly and bring to a boil. Stir in the tomato, basil, and pepper. Lower the heat and simmer for 7 to 8 minutes, or until the vegetables are tender. Set aside until the turkey is grilled.

Remove the turkey from the marinade and grill for 2 to 3 minutes on each side, positioning the grill 4 to 5 inches from the heat.

Transfer the *cacciatore* sauce to an oval serving dish and overlap the grilled medallions down the center. Sprinkle with parsley.

Fresh Cranberry Relish

Makes 2 cups

Once you've tried fresh cranberry relish, you'll never go back to the canned version.

2 cups fresh cranberries, washed

Juice and rind of 1 orange

1 cup water

¼ cup sugar

Pinch ground cinnamon

1 sprig fresh rosemary

Place the cranberries in a 2-quart saucepan and add the remaining ingredients. Bring to a boil, lower the heat, cover, and simmer for 5 to 6 minutes, or until the cranberries pop.

Smoking

• •

Before the days of canning and freezing, smoking was a way of preserving fish, meat, and poultry. Most food was brined and then cold-smoked at temperatures between 90° and 120°F. for long periods of time. This technique removed most of the moisture and changed the texture of the food.

Today's backyard smokers will both cook the food and at the same time give it a nice smoky flavor. Brining isn't necessary because the smoking temperature (195°F.) is high enough to destroy bacteria and molds. The combination of the heat, the hardwood smoke, and the moisture from the liquid in the water pan results in food with a penetrating flavor and a juicy texture.

Most smokers have a bulletlike shape and are built pretty much the same way. They consist of a firebox, which holds the charcoal or hardwood chunks, above which is suspended a water pan and one or two racks, which hold the food, and finally a hood. On one side is a door for replenishing the charcoal and small vents, usually at the top and bottom, which open and close for adjusting the heat. Some smokers use gas or electricity as fuel instead of hardwood or charcoal, but their design is essentially the same as that of the charcoal smoker.

For specific directions for lighting your smoker, consult your manufacturer's instructions.

Hints for Smoking

Know your fire: Check the temperature in the smoker every so often (it must stay low), but don't become a fanatic. Every time you lift the hood on the smoker, heat escapes, and it takes at least 15 to 20 minutes for the fire to build up again. This adds considerably to the total cooking time. That's probably why so many pots are sold today with glass covers.

If the smoking time is less than 2 hours, as it is with fish, you can use wood chips, but if you're smoking a piece of meat that requires 4 to 5 hours, you'll need large chunks of wood.

Soak wood chips for about an hour and drain off the liquid. Place the chips on the hot coals or in a fire box, and follow the smoking directions for each type of food.

Depending on the type of wood chips you use, you'll get a slightly different taste. Hickory or mesquite tend to give a smoky flavor, while apple or cherry woods instill a fruity one. Grapevine cuttings give food a slightly winey flavor, and adding orange, lemon, or lime peels to the fire lends a faint citrus one.

The choice of woods is almost endless. Make sure, however, that if you use wood from the backyard, it hasn't been sprayed with chemicals.

The liquid of choice need not be water. Use wine, beer, vinegar, or even cola in the water pan.

If a sizzling sound comes from the smoker, it usually means that the water pan needs to be refilled. When you do this, add some charcoal through the access door if your smoker has one.

242

Grilling
with
Chef
George
Hirsch

Fish can also be smoked by the hot-smoked method: cooked fish is placed in the smoker for a few minutes and infused on the surface with the flavor from the smoke.

Always read your manufacturer's instructions very carefully and keep them handy so you can refer to them

Smoked Shrimp

Makes 4 entree servings or 6 appetizer servings

These make great hors d'oeuvres, especially when grilled over cherry wood.

Indirect cooking

1 pound large shrimp (16 to 20 per pound)

1 cup Grilling Vinaigrette (page 144)

2 tablespoons cane syrup or dark corn syrup

Strong mustard

Do not peel the shrimp. Combine the vinaigrette and the cane syrup in a nonreactive bowl and marinate the shrimp for 1 hour in the refrigerator. Place the shrimp on a grill grid or thread onto skewers and smoke for 10 to 12 minutes. Serve with mustard.

Smoked Mako

Makes 4 servings

Indirect
cooking

Mako is one of the more popular species of shark and has the look and taste of swordfish. Soaking it in a mixture of water and lemon juice will eliminate any ammonia odor.

3 cups water

Juice of 1 lemon

About 1 pound 1-inch-thick mako steak

1 cup Grilling Vinaigrette (page 144)

2 tablespoons dried basil

1 teaspoon dried oregano

1 teaspoon Tabasco sauce

Dipping Sauce

1 cup mayonnaise

8 cloves Caramelized Garlic (page 111)

1 tablespoon minced garlic

1 tablespoon grated Parmesan cheese

Combine the water and lemon juice in a shallow bowl. Place the mako steak in the mixture and soak for 1 hour in the refrigerator. Drain well.

Combine the vinaigrette, basil, oregano, and Tabasco in a nonreactive bowl and add the mako steak. Marinate for 1 hour in the refrigerator, turning the steak once or twice. Smoke the mako for 45 to 50 minutes. Chill to serve.

244

Grilling
with
Chef
George
Hirsch

To make the dipping sauce, combine all of the ingredients in a small bowl and stir well.

Smoked Tuna

Makes 4 servings

Tuna is a good choice for smoking because it has a high fat content. It is especially tasty with an Oriental-style dipping sauce. Of course, I'm partial to Montauk tuna caught off the coast of Long Island.

1 cup Grilling Vinaigrette (page 144)

1 tablespoon chopped fresh ginger

1 teaspoon soy sauce

½ teaspoon sesame oil

About 1 pound 1-inch-thick tuna steak

Dipping Sauce

½ cup hoisin sauce

¼ cup catsup

2 tablespoons soy sauce

Combine the vinaigrette, ginger, soy sauce, and sesame oil in a nonreactive bowl. Add the tuna steak and marinate for 1 hour in the refrigerator, turning the tuna once or twice. Smoke the tuna for 45 to 50 minutes. Chill to serve.

To make the dipping sauce, combine all of the ingredients in a small bowl and mix well.

Smoked Oysters

Makes 4 entree servings or 6 appetizer servings

Indirect
cooking

This dish is a smoked version of oysters Rockefeller. It makes a great first course.

1 cup Grilling Vinaigrette (page 144)

2 tablespoons sambucca

2 dozen oysters, shucked and left on the half-shell

One 10-ounce package frozen chopped spinach

Dipping Sauce

¼ cup catsup

¼ cup chili sauce

Juice of 1 lemon

2 tablespoons grated horseradish

2 tablespoons hoisin sauce

2 teaspoons Tabasco sauce

Combine the vinaigrette and sambucca in a nonreactive bowl and marinate the oysters for 1 hour in the refrigerator. Cook the spinach according to the package directions and squeeze out any liquid. Remove the oysters from the marinade and cover them with the spinach. Smoke the oysters for 20 minutes. Serve hot.

To make the dipping sauce, combine all of the ingredients in a small bowl and mix well.

246

Grilling
with
Chef
George
Hirsch

Smoked Trout

Makes 4 servings

Trout purchased in fish markets are farmed in various parts of the country. They're mild tasting, so the horseradish in the dipping sauce adds a welcome bit of zip.

Indirect
cooking

I cup Grilling Vinaigrette (page 144)

2 tablespoons maple syrup

6 trout fillets, 4 to 6 ounces each

Dipping Sauce

I cup mayonnaise

2 tablespoons grated horseradish

I tablespoon maple syrup

Combine the vinaigrette and maple syrup in a nonreactive bowl and marinate the trout fillets for 1 hour in the refrigerator. Smoke the trout for 30 minutes. Serve chilled.

To make the dipping sauce, combine all of the ingredients in a small bowl and mix well.

Smoked Salmon

Salmon, one of the most popular types of fish on the grill, is also a favorite for smoking because of its rich flavor. Chill the salmon after smoking; serve with whole-grain bread.

> **1 cup Grilling Vinaigrette (page 144)**
>
> **1 tablespoon corn syrup**
>
> **1 teaspoon Tabasco sauce**
>
> **2 tablespoons coarsely chopped fresh dill**
>
> **1 salmon fillet, about 1 pound**
>
> ### Dipping Sauce
>
> **1 cup sour cream**
>
> **2 tablespoons mustard**
>
> **2 tablespoons chopped scallion**
>
> **1 tablespoon minced fresh dill**

Combine the vinaigrette, corn syrup, Tabasco, and dill in a nonreactive bowl and marinate the salmon for 1 hour in the refrigerator. Smoke the salmon for 45 to 50 minutes. Serve chilled.

To make the dipping sauce, combine all of the ingredients in a small bowl and mix well.

248

Grilling
with
Chef
George
Hirsch

Smoked Tuna
with Tomato Relish

Use your smoker for this recipe, or transform your covered grill into a smoker by adding soaked wood chips to the fire. You can substitute mako, swordfish, or catfish for the tuna.

Indirect
cooking

> I lemon slice and I teaspoon dried thyme for soaking wood chips
>
> ½ cup olive oil
>
> 2 tablespoons white wine
>
> Juice of 2 lemons
>
> ½ teaspoon dried basil
>
> ½ tablespoon dried thyme
>
> ¼ teaspoon Tabasco sauce
>
> Four 5-ounce tuna fillets from the loin
>
> Salad greens
>
> I recipe Tomato Relish (recipe follows)

Soak apple or pecan wood chips for 1 hour in water with lemon slices and thyme. Preheat the smoker for 20 minutes.

(continued)

249

Whisk the oil, wine, lemon juice, basil, thyme, and Tabasco in a shallow dish. Marinate the tuna fillets in this mixture for at least 1 hour, refrigerated.

Remove the tuna from the marinade. Place the marinade in an ovenproof pan, and place the pan in the smoker's water pan. Place the tuna on the smoker's grid, close the cover, and smoke for 30 to 35 minutes. Remove the tuna and let it cool. Serve chilled and sliced over greens, with tomato relish on the side.

Tomato Relish

Makes about 2 cups

4 plum tomatoes, seeded and chopped

2 peaches, nectarines, or plums, chopped

2 tablespoons chopped scallion

2 tablespoons chopped celery

½ cup diced unpeeled zucchini

I cup cooked black beans

2 tablespoons olive oil

Salt and pepper to taste

250

Grilling

with

Chef

George

Hirsch

Combine the tomato, peach, scallion, celery, zucchini, black beans, and olive oil in a small bowl and stir well. Season with salt and pepper.

Smoked
Pork Tenderloin

Makes 6 to 8 servings

Indirect
cooking

These tenderloins get a lot of flavor from the pork dry rub. They get a second burst of flavor from the apple wood in the smoker. Finally, they're served with Smoked Apples and Raisins (page 253). It doesn't get much better. Don't trim off the fat from the tenderloins because it will help baste them during the smoking. And remember to plan ahead, because the meat must be aged in the refrigerator for about 8 hours before smoking.

Two 1½-pound pork tenderloins

½ cup Pork Dry Rub (page 156)

Apple Pork Water

2 cups water

2 cups apple juice

2 bay leaves

½ onion

1 rib celery

Rub the dry rub all over the pork tenderloins and refrigerate for 8 hours.

Prepare the smoker with charcoal, or preheat it if it's electric. Presoak chunks of apple wood in water for 2 hours and place them on the fuel grate.

Smoking

(continued)

Combine the water, apple juice, bay leaves, onion, and celery. When the charcoal become gray or when the lava rocks are hot, add the apple pork water to the water pan. If your smoker doesn't have a water pan, use a loaf pan for the water.

Place the pork tenderloin on the grill, cover, and do not open for 1 hour. Check the level in the water pan and refill if necessary. Cover and cook 30 minutes longer. Remove the pork from the grill and let it rest for 15 to 20 minutes before slicing.

Grilling
with
Chef
George
Hirsch

Smoked Apples
and Raisins

Makes 4 servings

Use Granny Smith apples or any other tart green apples. Baking apples will fall apart.

4 **Granny Smith apples**

2 **tablespoons sugar**

Juice and zest of 1 lemon

¼ **cup apple juice**

1 **tablespoon margarine, melted**

1 **tablespoon brandy**

1 **cinnamon stick**

Prepare the smoker.

Peel the apples, remove the cores, and cut the apples into quarters. Place the apples in an ovenproof baking dish. In a small bowl, combine the sugar, lemon juice and zest, apple juice, margarine, and brandy, and mix well. Pour the mixture over the apples, toss well to combine, and tuck the cinnamon stick under the apples.

Cover the dish with aluminum foil and poke several holes in it with a sharp knife. Place the dish in the smoker for 1 hour. Serve with pork or poultry.

Smoked Pork Shoulder
a.k.a. Carolina Barbecue

Indirect cooking

We have many different types of barbecue in our country. Shredded pork barbecue takes hours to smoke and is mindless cooking, a good thing to make during colder weather in the North.

Carolina-style vinegar barbecue sauce is slightly sour compared to the molasses- and sugar-based red barbecue sauces so popular in the Southwest and North.

One 9- to 11-pound pork shoulder

2 tablespoons sea salt

1 tablespoon coarsely ground black pepper

1 tablespoon paprika

Soft white hamburger rolls

Carolina Barbecue Sauce (recipe follows)

Prepare a water smoker for 10 hours (pages 242–243). Season the pork shoulders with sea salt, pepper, and paprika, and smoke for 6 hours at 195°F. After 2 hours, add chunks of soaked hickory to the smoker. When the meat is cooked, remove it from the smoker and let it sit for about an hour. Slice the meat off the bone, then chop it into shreds. Serve on hamburger buns with Carolina Barbecue Sauce.

254

Grilling
with
Chef
George
Hirsch

Carolina
Barbecue Sauce #1

Makes about 1 cup

Carolina-style barbecue is traditionally on the sour side. If you want a sweeter sauce, add ½ cup brown sugar and a pinch of ground mace to either recipe.

Here are two versions. The first is the more traditional sauce, the second contains tomatoes, which the more authentic sauce does not.

½ **cup red-wine vinegar**

2 **tablespoons peanut oil**

¼ **cup Dijon mustard**

2 **tablespoons Worcestershire sauce**

1 **tablespoon sweet paprika**

¼ **teaspoon Tabasco sauce**

Combine all of the ingredients in a nonreactive saucepan and bring to a boil. Lower the heat and simmer for 10 minutes.

Carolina Barbecue Sauce # 2

Makes about 2 1/2 cups

I cup tomato puree

1/2 cup finely chopped onion

I cup red-wine vinegar

1/4 teaspoon cayenne

Combine all of the ingredients in a nonreactive saucepan and bring to a boil. Lower the heat and simmer for 8 to 10 minutes.

Maple-Smoked Turkey Legs

Makes 8 servings

These days, if you want turkey, you don't have to buy a whole bird, since parts are readily available in supermarkets. You can use turkey breasts in this recipe, but I like to use the legs because they have a lot of fat, which keeps the meat moist. The trick is to keep the temperature at around 195°F.—you want the meat to smoke, and it can't do that at a higher temperature. If you don't have a smoker, you can use your grill, providing it has a hood.

For an interesting flavor, pour the marinade into the smoker's water pan and add 12 ounces of ginger ale, cider, or cola.

½ **cup maple syrup**

½ **cup fresh orange juice**

2 **tablespoons paprika**

½ **teaspoon dried sage**

¼ **teaspoon ground nutmeg**

⅛ **teaspoon ground allspice**

Salt and pepper to taste

8 **turkey legs**

Prepare the smoker 1 hour before cooking, preferably with half hickory and half apple wood, both of which have been presoaked for an hour.

Combine the maple syrup, orange juice, paprika, sage, nutmeg, allspice, salt, and pepper in a shallow dish and mix well. Marinate the turkey legs in this mixture for 8 to 10 hours in the refrigerator. Cook the turkey legs at 195°F. for 3 to 4 hours, or until tender.

Long Island Duck
Pacific Rim Style

Because of their high fat content, ducks smoke exceptionally well, and the flesh is constantly being basted by the fat. Don't rush the smoking procedure. The slower the ducks are roasted, the more fat will be rendered. To serve, remove the breasts from the carcasses and separate the legs and thighs from the body cavities.

Two 4½-pound ducks, split in half

2 cups Pacific Rim Marinade (page 148)

1 cup pineapple juice

Prepare a charcoal fire on one side of the grill about 4 hours before you want to serve the duck. Add presoaked apple, cherry, or pecan wood to the hot coals. The temperature should be 195°F. Do not use lighter fluid to start the fire because it may impart its flavor to the food.

Marinate the ducks in Pacific Rim marinade for 8 hours. Place the ducks on the side of the grill without the fire. Add the pineapple juice to the marinade and place it in a water pan under the ducks. Close the hood and cook the ducks for 2 hours. Remove the ducks, wrap them in aluminum foil, and cook them for 45 minutes more. To crisp up the skins, remove the water pan and place the ducks on the grill, skin sides down, for about 15 to 20 minutes over a hotter fire (about 350°F.), without lowering the hood.

258

Grilling
with
Chef
George
Hirsch

Drinks

Though it's easy to reach for a beer while you're grilling, there may be times when you want something hot, or sweet, or just plain delicious. Making drinks is a great way to get children involved in cooking—just choose a recipe that's easy to prepare.

Egg Cream

Makes I serving

An egg cream is a New York City soda-fountain concoction that became popular in the fifties. It contains neither egg nor cream but when properly mixed, produces a foamlike head similar to beaten egg whites.

> ¼ **cup chocolate syrup**
> **I cup milk, chilled**
> **One I2-ounce glass filled with ice**
> **Seltzer (not club soda)**

Pour the chocolate syrup and milk into a shaker glass and shake for 30 seconds. Pour into the ice-filled glass and top off with seltzer.

Blueberry Cooler

Makes 6 servings

The combination of blueberries and cranberries produces a drink that's a lovely shade of purple. The addition of lemonade adds just the right touch of tartness.

1 pint blueberries

1 cup ice

2 cups cranberry juice

4 cups lemonade

One 12-ounce bottle ginger ale

Place the blueberries and ice in a blender and blend for 20 seconds. Add the cranberry juice and blend for 15 seconds. Add the lemonade and blend for 15 seconds. Fill six glasses three-quarters full and top off with ginger ale.

Iced Cappuccino

Makes 4 servings

For iced-coffee drinkers, iced cappuccino is heaven. No drink is more refreshing on a hot summer's afternoon.

2 tablespoons sugar

1 teaspoon unsweetened cocoa

2 cups milk

2 cups cold espresso

Ice

1 cup sweetened whipped cream

Ground cinnamon or cocoa for garnish

In a 6-cup pitcher, combine the sugar and cocoa. Stir in the milk and espresso and mix well. Fill four tall glasses with ice, and add the espresso mixture. Top with 2 tablespoons whipped cream and dust with cinnamon or cocoa.

Hot Buttered Tea

Although the rum is optional, it adds fragrance as well as body to cinnamon tea. Perfect sipping for those who like to grill in cold weather.

> 4 cups boiling water
>
> 4 tea bags
>
> 4 tablespoons sugar
>
> 3 to 4 tablespoons unsalted butter
>
> 2 cinnamon sticks
>
> I cup fresh orange juice
>
> ¼ cup rum (optional)
>
> Fresh mint leaves for garnish

In a large bowl or teapot, combine the boiling water, tea bags, sugar, butter, and cinnamon sticks. Brew for 5 minutes and remove the tea bags and cinnamon sticks. Stir in the orange juice and rum. Pour into glass cups and garnish with mint.

262

Grilling
with
Chef
George
Hirsch

Ginger Ale

Makes 4 servings

Once you make ginger ale from scratch, you'll have trouble going back to the stuff in the bottle.

>   **2 tablespoons grated fresh ginger**
>
>   **Rind of 2 lemons**
>
>   **2 tablespoons sugar**
>
>   **2 tablespoons honey**
>
>   **I cup boiling water**
>
>   **I quart club soda**

Place the ginger, lemon rind, sugar, and honey in a bowl and add the boiling water. Cool, refrigerate for 8 hours or overnight, and strain. When ready to serve, add the club soda.

Sun Tea

Makes 8 servings

Traditionally, sun tea is brewed in the sun, but if the sun isn't shining, it brews just as well in the refrigerator.

8 tea bags

3 quarts water

Sugar (optional)

Ice

Lemon slices

Place the tea bags in a 1-gallon glass jug and add the water. Cover and place in the sun for 6 hours. Sweeten to taste with sugar, if desired. Add ice and sliced lemons.

Variations

Mint sun tea	add 8 mint leaves
Basil sun tea	add 6 basil leaves
Orange sun tea	add 1 sliced orange
Lemonade sun tea	mix equal parts iced tea and lemonade

Lemonade

Makes 8 servings

What's a barbecue without a tall pitcher of frosty lemonade? To get more juice out of the lemons, roll them back and forth on a hard surface before slicing.

6 to 8 lemons, sliced and seeded

2 cups sugar

1 pint hot water

Cold water and ice

Mash the lemon slices in a 1-gallon pitcher. Add the sugar and hot water, stir, and let sit until the mixture cools. Add enough cold water and ice to fill the pitcher, and stir well.

Iced Café au Lait

Chicory coffee is a New Orleans favorite. To make cold devil's coffee, add ¼ cup brandy and 2 tablespoons Triple Sec to the blender.

3 cups fresh-brewed chicory coffee, cold

2 cups half-and-half

2 tablespoons brown sugar, or to taste

2 cups crushed ice

Place the coffee, half-and-half, and brown sugar in a blender and blend until frothy. Pour over ice.

266

Grilling

with

Chef

George

Hirsch

Desserts

• •

Now that it's been demonstrated that so many other parts of the menu can be cooked on the grill, why go back into the house to make dessert, especially if the fire is still going? (Of course, if it's easier to make desserts early in the morning, they can be made in the kitchen.)

Many desserts here are fruit based, a refreshing way to end a meal of grilled foods. We also give a range of sauces that can be used with ice cream, cake, and fruit.

Banana Boats

Bananas have never tasted so good! Place them on the grill when you sit down to eat the main course, and they should be cooked, cooled, and ready by the time you finish. Use large yellow bananas with the barest green tips. If the bananas have any brown spots, they're too ripe. For true decadence, top the bananas with a dollop of sweetened whipped cream and some chopped pecans just before serving.

> **6 bananas**
>
> **Three 1-ounce chocolate bars, broken into small pieces, or**
>
> > **6 tablespoons mini-chocolate chips**
>
> **2 cups mini-marshmallows**
>
> **Six 12-inch squares aluminum foil**

Split the bananas down the inner sides, but do not remove the peels. Spread the peels apart and evenly place the chocolate pieces and marshmallows between the bananas and the peels. Bring the edges of the peels together as closely as possible and wrap each banana in foil.

Grill the bananas for 4 to 5 minutes; turn them and move them to the cooler edge of the grill for 4 to 5 minutes.

268

Grilling
with
Chef
George
Hirsch

Blueberry Buckle

Makes 8 servings

Don't be limited by blueberries in this recipe. Use whatever fruit is in season—strawberries, raspberries, or cherries. When using fresh fruit, substitute orange juice for the liquid. If you are doubtful about making desserts on the grill, this is the one to begin with.

Grill temperature

high

One 1-pound can unsweetened blueberries, packed in juice

1 ½ cups sugar

¾ cup buttermilk biscuit mix

½ cup water

Pinch ground cinnamon

Pinch ground nutmeg

2 tablespoons butter, in small pieces

Vanilla ice cream or sweetened whipped cream

Drain the blueberries, reserving ½ cup juice. Place the blueberries, the reserved juice, and ½ cup sugar in a 10-inch nonstick skillet and stir well. Place on the grill, bring the mixture to a boil, and boil for 1½ to 2 minutes, stirring constantly.

Mix the biscuit mix with the remaining 1 cup sugar, water, cinnamon, and nutmeg. Stir well and drop by teaspoonsful over the berries. Cook, uncovered, for 8 to 10 minutes. Dot with butter, lower the grill hood (or cover the pan with aluminum foil), and cook for 5 to 8 minutes. Serve with vanilla ice cream or whipped cream.

Peaches
with Mascarpone

This delightful way to serve peaches doesn't require the use of the grill, but it's a great way to end a grilled meal. If you can't locate mascarpone, combine ½ soft cup cream cheese, ½ cup heavy cream, and ¼ cup sugar. Slices of angel food cake, sponge cake, or pound cake can be substituted for the ladyfingers.

> 6 large, ripe peaches
>
> 2 cups port
>
> Juice and zest of 1 orange
>
> 1 cup mascarpone
>
> 2 tablespoons sugar
>
> 1 cup heavy cream, whipped
>
> 18 lady fingers
>
> 6 sprigs fresh mint for garnish

Slice and pit the peaches, removing the skins if desired. In a nonreactive bowl, combine the port, orange juice, and zest. Add the peaches and marinate for 1 hour. Whip the mascarpone with the sugar and fold in the whipped cream. To serve, remove the peaches from the marinade and arrange on a serving platter. Arrange the lady fingers around the outside and top with dollops of the mascarpone mixture. Garnish with mint.

270

Grilling
with
Chef
George
Hirsch

Bananas Foster

Makes 8 servings

Bananas Foster is a New Orleans treat and, when made tableside in a restaurant, is a real show-biz extravaganza. Add some chocolate chips or nuts, if you so desire, but don't forget the vanilla ice cream.

Grill
temperature

medium-low

8 bananas, ripe but still firm

½ cup brown sugar

¼ cup granulated sugar

1 teaspoon ground cinnamon

½ teaspoon ground nutmeg

4 tablespoons (½ stick) butter

Eight 12-inch squares aluminum foil

Vanilla ice cream

Slice the bananas along the inner curves, leaving the peels on. In a small bowl, combine the brown and granulated sugars with the cinnamon and nutmeg; stir well. Spread about 4 teaspoons of the mixture between the bananas and the peels, and top each with ½ tablespoon butter. Wrap the bananas securely in foil and place on the grill for 10 to 12 minutes, turning several times. Serve with vanilla ice cream.

Apple-Raisin
Bread Pudding

Makes 10 to 12 servings

I like to use day-old French bread in bread pudding because it has more flavor than the gummy white kind. Cinnamon-raisin bread or sweet rolls can also be substituted for part of the bread. Although one doesn't usually think of baking a bread pudding on a grill, it's a homey dish that goes well after a grilling feast. Puree some strawberries with sugar for a sauce or, if you're in the mood, serve it with Louisiana Bourbon Sauce.

2 Granny Smith or baking apples

Vegetable oil

3 to 4 cups cubed dry French bread

½ cup chopped walnuts or pecans

½ cup raisins, plumped in 1 cup hot water for 5 minutes

2 tablespoons butter, melted

4 cups milk

8 eggs

1 cup sugar

2 tablespoons vanilla extract

1 tablespoon ground cinnamon

½ tablespoon ground nutmeg

Louisiana Bourbon Sauce (page 283)

272

Grilling
with
Chef
George
Hirsch

Peel and core the apples. Slice them into rounds, brush them with vegetable oil, and grill them for 2 minutes on each side. Remove the apples and chop coarsely.

In a medium bowl, combine the apples, bread, nuts, raisins, and melted butter. Spoon into a buttered 10- by 3-inch cake pan or a 10-inch black iron skillet.

In a separate bowl, combine the milk, eggs, sugar, vanilla, cinnamon, and nutmeg, and beat with a whisk until well blended. Slowly pour over the bread mixture. Poke the bread down so that it's completely covered with the milk mixture and let it sit for 10 to 15 minutes.

Place a pan larger than the cake pan or skillet on the grill, and place the pan holding the bread pudding inside. Immediately fill the outer pan with enough hot water so that it comes up 1 inch on the sides of the bread-pudding pan. Lower the hood and bake for 30 minutes on medium heat (375°F.). Remove the pan from the water bath, reduce the temperature to low (325°F.), and bake for 25 minutes. Remove the pan and allow the bread pudding to set for 2 hours before removing it from the pan. Serve with bourbon sauce.

Filo Pecan Pie

Makes 8 servings

Filo Pecan Pie is a spin-off of traditional pecan pie. Instead of using a pastry crust, the filling is placed on sheets of filo, and the tops are twisted to make it a closed pie. This version is not as sticky and sweet as traditional pecan pie. The pie can also be baked in a conventional oven at 350°F. for 40 to 45 minutes.

> 4 eggs
>
> I egg yolk
>
> I cup light corn syrup
>
> ¾ cup sugar
>
> 2 teaspoons vanilla extract
>
> ½ teaspoon fresh lemon juice
>
> ½ teaspoon salt
>
> ½ pound pecans
>
> 8 sheets filo pastry
>
> ¼ pound (I stick) butter, melted

In a medium bowl, combine the eggs, egg yolk, corn syrup, sugar, vanilla, lemon juice, and salt, and whisk until well combined. Stir in the pecans.

Unfold the filo sheets and lay them on a flat surface. To prevent the filo from drying out too quickly, cover them with plastic wrap and a damp towel. Remove one sheet of filo, brush it with melted butter, and place it in a

274

Grilling
with
Chef
George
Hirsch

buttered 10-inch cake pan. Repeat with the remaining sheets, placing them one on top of the other. Pour the filling into the pan, gently gather the excess filo in the center, and twist carefully to make a cover for the pie. Bake on the grill with the hood down for 40 minutes.

Ricotta Balls

Makes 5 to 6 dozen

Ricotta balls are almost like *beignets* (French doughnuts), and the addition of the cheese makes them very custardy inside. Cook them on the side burner of a grill and you'll keep the kitchen clean and cool. After you cook a few, taste them and adjust the temperature of the oil, if necessary. When they cook too quickly, they'll be raw inside, and if they cook at too low a temperature, they'll be oily.

Whenever deep-frying, take extra care not to leave hot oil unattended, especially when there are children nearby. And take extra precautions that oil doesn't spill onto an open flame and cause a flare-up.

2½ pounds self-rising cake flour (preferably Presto)

14 to 16 eggs

3 pounds ricotta

1 cup granulated sugar

Hot oil for frying

Confectioners' sugar

(continued)

Grill temperature

high

275

Desserts

In a large bowl, combine the cake flour, 14 eggs, ricotta, and granulated sugar. Stir well, and add an additional egg or two if the mixture falls apart. Set the mixture aside for 20 minutes.

Pour several inches of oil into a deep pot or skillet and heat on a side burner of the grill to 350°F. Using 2 tablespoons, pick up some of the mixture with one spoon and drop it into the hot fat with the second spoon.

Cook until the ricotta balls are golden brown on all sides. Remove them and drain on paper towels. Roll each ball in confectioners' sugar while still warm, and once again when cool.

Fresh Strawberry Crisp with Cinnamon-Crisp Topping

Makes 4 servings

This is an impressive dessert that looks like it's a lot harder and more time-consuming to make than it actually is. The cinnamon-crisp topping can be used to top any pudding or pie.

2 cups sliced fresh strawberries

¼ cup sugar

1 tablespoon maple syrup

Four 3-inch graham-cracker tart shells

Cinnamon-Crisp Topping

¼ cup all-purpose flour

¼ cup sugar

1 teaspoon ground cinnamon

¼ teaspoon ground nutmeg

2 tablespoons butter, cut into small pieces

Whipped cream

In a small heavy saucepan, combine ½ cup sliced strawberries, the sugar, and the maple syrup. Stir well and simmer for 4 to 5 minutes on side burner or conventional stovetop. Cool and fill the tart shells evenly with the mixture.

For the topping, in a small bowl, combine the flour, sugar, cinnamon, and nutmeg, and mix well. Add the butter and mix until large crumbs form. Do not overmix. Place the mixture in a nonstick skillet and toast on the grill until crunchy. Cool.

Top the tarts with the remaining strawberries and the Cinnamon-Crisp Topping. Serve with whipped cream.

Chocolate Fondue

Makes 4 servings

Chocolate fondue is a chocoholic's dream of dying and going to heaven. If you melt the chocolate in a colorful enamel-on-steel pot, you can serve the fondue in it.

> **8 ounces semisweet or bittersweet chocolate**
>
> **I cup heavy cream**
>
> **I tablespoon butter**
>
> **I tablespoon brandy**
>
> **Fruit (strawberries, apples, bananas, pears, etc., cut into bite-size pieces)**
>
> **Sponge cake or angel food cake, cubed**

Chop the chocolate into small pieces and place in a medium saucepan on the grill over medium-low heat. Allow the chocolate to melt slightly. In a separate pan, heat the cream over high heat until it comes to a boil. Slowly pour the cream over the chocolate, and stir until completely mixed and smooth. Stir in the butter and then the brandy.

Using fondue forks, dip pieces of fruit or cake into the fondue.

Strawberry Pizza

Makes 4 servings

Add a dash of cinnamon to the sugar for a new twist. Blueberries or raspberries can be used instead of strawberries.

Grill
temperature

medium-high

1 recipe Pizza Dough (page 96)

¼ cup olive oil or melted butter

2 tablespoons butter, melted

¼ cup sugar

1 cup mascarpone or whipped cream cheese

1 cup sliced strawberries

Divide the pizza dough into two equal portions, and stretch each into a 10-inch circle. Brush with olive oil or butter, place on the grill, and cook 2 minutes. Turn the pizzas over and cook 2 minutes longer. Remove the pizzas from the grill and immediately brush them with butter and sprinkle them heavily with sugar. Spread each pizza with mascarpone to within ¼ inch of the edge. Arrange half the sliced strawberries on top of each pizza.

Strawberry Tart

The pink whipped cream is as light as a cloud, and makes this dessert a real show-stopper. This is a good recipe for children to make and was created by my daughter Dori.

½ cup maple syrup

½ cup granulated sugar

1 cup sliced strawberries

Four 3½-inch graham-cracker tart shells

1 cup heavy cream

½ cup confectioners' sugar

6 drops red food coloring

¼ teaspoon vanilla extract

In a small saucepan, combine the maple syrup and the granulated sugar and cook on the grill for 5 minutes. Stir in half the strawberries and allow the mixture to cool for 5 minutes. Stir in the remaining strawberries. When the mixture is completely cool, divide it among the tart shells.

Beat the cream until soft peaks form, adding the sugar gradually, and then the food coloring and vanilla. Pile on top of the tarts.

Butterscotch Sauce

Makes I cup

Butterscotch sauce is traditionally poured over vanilla ice cream, but give it a chance over rum raisin and you may never go back to vanilla.

I cup packed brown sugar

½ cup cane syrup or corn syrup

6 tablespoons (¾ stick) unsalted butter

½ cup heavy cream

¼ teaspoon vanilla extract

In a heavy saucepan, combine the brown sugar, cane syrup, and butter. Bring to a boil over the grill, stirring constantly. Lower the heat and simmer for 1 minute. Remove from the heat and stir in the heavy cream and vanilla. Serve warm or cold.

Grill temperature

medium-low, then low

281

Desserts

Caramel Sauce

Makes about 1 cup

Drizzle this sauce over cream puffs or chocolate ice cream.

1 cup sugar

2 tablespoons butter

¼ cup heavy cream

Juice and zest of ½ orange

In a heavy saucepan, heat the sugar over the grill, stirring constantly, until it melts and becomes liquid. As soon as the sugar turns light brown, stir in the butter and simmer the mixture for 15 to 20 seconds. Slowly add the cream and simmer for 2 minutes over low heat. Stir the orange juice and zest.

282

Grilling
with
Chef
George
Hirsch

Louisiana Bourbon Sauce

Makes 1 ¼ cups

In parts of Louisiana, one wouldn't dream of eating bread pudding without a topping of bourbon sauce.

Grill temperature

low

½ cup sugar

1 teaspoon cornstarch

2 egg yolks

1 cup milk

¼ cup bourbon

½ teaspoon vanilla extract

In a small bowl, combine the sugar and cornstarch. Add the egg yolks and stir well. In a heavy saucepan heat the milk to a simmer over the grill and stir ¼ cup of the milk into the yolk mixture. Stir well and pour the mixture into the pot. Heat slowly, stirring constantly, until the mixture thickens. Stir in the bourbon and vanilla.

Fruit Sauce

Makes about 2 cups

Grill temperature

low

With a package of frozen fruit in the freezer, dessert is never far away. Use this fruit sauce over melon balls and kiwi, or toasted pound cake and vanilla ice cream.

One 12-ounce package frozen strawberries or blueberries, with juice

1 cup sugar

Juice and zest of ½ orange

Combine the frozen fruit, sugar, orange juice, and zest in a heavy saucepan and simmer over the grill for 5 to 7 minutes. Cool, place in a blender, and puree. Chill before serving.

Index